Mel Bay Presents

The Glengarry Collection

The Highland Fiddle Music of Aonghas Grant

Volume 1

By Aonghas Grant
with Barbara McOwen, Laura Risk
& Peggy Duesenberry

Edited by Barbara McOwen

164 Slow Airs, Marches, Strathspeys, Reels, Jigs & Hornpipes
with
Stories, History and Photographs

Includes Bowings, Gracings, Variants, Tempos and Chords

Cover photo of fiddle by Nate Silva.

1 2 3 4 5 6 7 8 9 0

Visit us on the Web at www.melbay.com — E-mail us at email@melbay.com

Aonghas Grant's Scotland

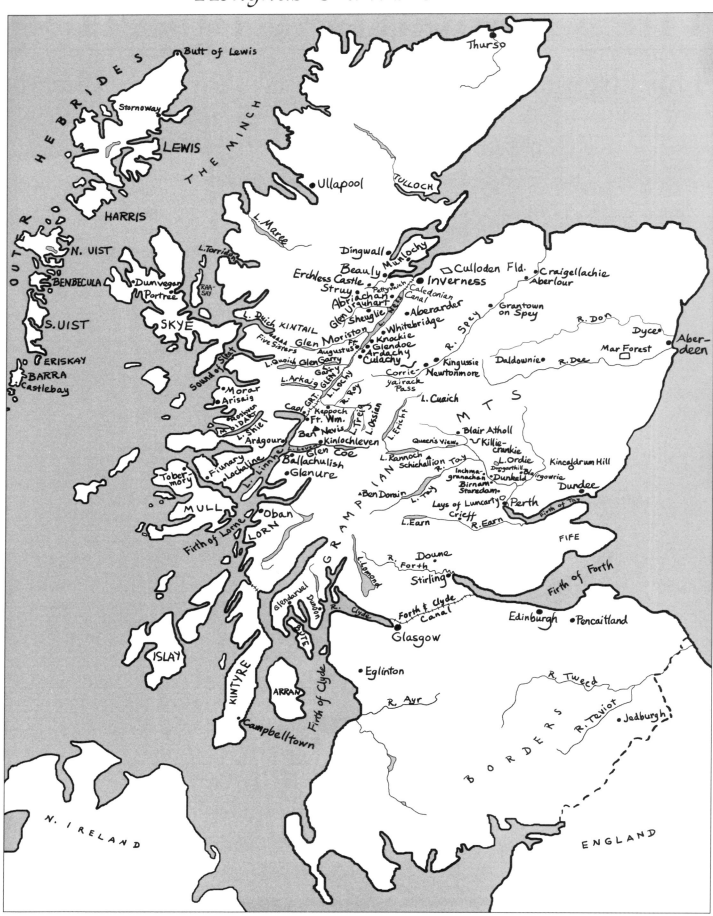

Table of Contents

Tune Listing

Acknowledgments

Thanks to all the composers and copyright holders who gave us permission to reprint tunes and seconds, the artists and photographers who allowed us to reproduce their work, and Aonghas' many students and friends that have written down his repertoire over the years.

We especially appreciate encouragement from Alastair J. Hardie and David H. Arnold in the early stages of this project. Thanks to Kate Dunlay, George Ruckert, Ken Perlman and Jan Tappan for advice and encouragement, and to everyone who looked through early drafts and offered suggestions, including Anne Hooper, Gregor Borland and Chris Stout.

Thanks to Cal Howard for digitizing Peggy's reel-to-reel tapes and to Nancy Bell for transcribing Aonghas' stories and tune histories from those recordings. Thanks to Tom Pixton, Kristin Grenara and Ryan McKasson for their artistic and computer expertise, Nate Silva for offering professional help with graphic design and photography, and Jill Newman and Julie Price at Mel Bay for their guidance. Thanks to Colleen Mohyde for donating professional expertise in publishing and to Marc Bolduc for his support.

We are grateful to Mairi MacMaster and Mary Ann Kennedy for expert help with the Gaelic.

Aonghas appreciates very much the early work done on transcriptions of tunes by his colleagues and students, especially Rosemary Stewart, Veronique Nelson, Nicola Patience and Val Bryan.

We are also grateful to all at the University of Stirling Heritage of Scotland Summer School, particularly Margery Stirling.

Thanks to Robert McOwen, who has supported this project in every way imaginable. We would especially like to acknowledge his financial support and his assistance with chords.

A special thanks to Moira MacLeod Grant, Angus R. Grant, Fiona Grant and Deirdre Grant Corser for their support of this project.

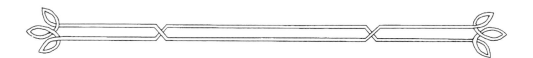

Made possible in part by a grant from
The New Hampshire Gathering of the Scottish Clans

Author's Preface

For over thirty years friends and others have said I should get a music book out. With the laid back attitude of the West Highlander I agreed and did nothing about it. My friend Barbara McOwen, whom I first met when I was a tutor at Stirling University Summer Schools, was the one who gave me the push. Barbara said she would take on the job, and so it began.

Like most traditional musicians I picked up all my tunes by ear. I only had to hear a tune once to have it. I think this ability to pick up a tune is becoming diluted, as most players can now read music. None of the fine old fiddlers I knew over half a century ago read music, but carried hundreds of tunes in their heads, four and six part pipe marches with their own style of bowing. The tape recorder, when it came on the scene, was a great help, but with players now hearing tunes from all over the world the old styles are in danger of becoming lost. In this book I have tried to convey the highland fiddle style I grew up with. I realise that most good players put their own imprint on a tune and why not, I do also.

I would like to say a grateful thanks to Barbara, Laura Risk and Peggy Duesenberry for all their hard work with the tunes and the bowings; to all my musicial friends and pupils for their help and encouragement over the years; to my wife Moira and our three musical children who have inspired me to keep playing and composing; and to my father who installed a love of music and song in me at an early age.

Aonghas Grant

Lochyside
Lochaber
25 October 2008

Editor's Preface

"Aonghas Grant needs a book." I first heard these words in 1984 when I attended the Stirling University Heritage of Scotland Summer School. The other fiddle tutors that year, Tom Anderson and Alastair Hardie, had fine books, recently published, and were now teaching from them. With Aonghas, however, the office was in a flurry each morning. "Could I get 12 copies of this, and 3 more of that. And here's a scrap with part of a tune on it, can anyone put the rest of the notes down? And what was that tune from yesterday, does anyone have a book with that tune in it?" The papers were flying.

It was no different fourteen years later when Aonghas came over to the States to teach at the New Hampshire Highland Games. The same papers were flying, and we heard the same refrain: "Aonghas Grant needs a book."

It occurred to me that I could do such a book for Aonghas. I can transcribe tunes, I'm used to presenting readable sheet music to all sorts of fiddlers, I have a large collection of Scottish fiddle books from which to draw not only raw material but also inspiration, and most of all I love Aonghas' repertoire, his way of playing the music, and the depth of his fiddling life – the stories, the history, the people, the land. I wanted to hear more, I wanted to know more, and very little of what Aonghas presented in his teaching was in any book. I approached him with the idea and he agreed we should collect his work so it could live on.

I began to seek out people who could work on this with me. I called my friend Peggy Duesenberry, who had been in Aonghas' course at Stirling that same year, and who had taped the entire two-week course in 1984 and again in 1988. By then she had her PhD in Ethnomusicology and was teaching at the Royal Scottish Academy of Music and Drama, and I was excited by the prospect of tapping both her scholastic grounding and her field experience. I also called David H. Arnold, a fiddle colleague who had struck up a particularly warm friendship with Aonghas and who was very interested in Aonghas' gracing style. After Dave had to drop out of the project for health reasons, Laura Risk enthusiastically took up the call and has accomplished a true *tour-de-force* transcription of Aonghas' complex improvisational ornamentation. This is the group that, with Aonghas at the head, has brought this ambitious, fascinating project to fruition.

As I write I also feel the presence of a few special people. My late great-aunt Maud helped finance my violin lessons in my teens, because she "loved the violin music." At the turn of the last century her uncles and cousins (newly emigrated from Scotland) had a fiddle band in Nebraska, and when they came to play for special occasions she would hide in her room because the music was so beautiful and she didn't want everyone to see her crying. My late father, James Roy Turner, who financed that trip to Stirling in 1984. He asked only "How much do you need and when do you need it?" My late violin teacher, Jack O'Brien, second fiddle in the renowned Griller Quartet. Of a passage in a Mozart concerto, he said, "Those are Scotch snaps." My late Scottish dance teacher, C. Stewart Smith, of Fife and San Francisco. In class one night long ago he said of the ubiquitous accordion recordings: "This is all violin music, you know."

It is a great honor to work with Aonghas, alongside Peggy and Laura, to set down part of Aonghas' multi-dimensional musical and narrative repertoire onto two-dimensional paper. It is my hope that this volume is worthy of Aonghas Grant's heritage and that it will find its place among the others in a 200-year-long line of finely-printed and much-fingered Scottish fiddle books.

Barbara McOwen
Arlington, Massachusetts
September 10, 2008

Using This Collection

Aonghas Grant has been learning tunes ever since he can remember and he is still actively increasing his repertoire. He is the direct inheritor of at least two long generations' worth of music: that of his own life span and that of his uncle's, who was born in the 1870s. Aonghas likes to compose tunes and he has also had a number of tunes written for him.

This collection focuses on the core of Aonghas' music: Highland fiddling, with its links to pipe tunes and Gaelic songs. Some of these tunes have never been published before, while others are available only in out-of-print books or in pipe settings. Some are easily available in printed form but are included because Aonghas has a very distinct and personal approach to their performance. Lastly, the collection includes tunes composed by Aonghas himself.

Sources: Aonghas has collected a large number of hand-written transcriptions of tunes in his repertoire. The earliest were made by his students at the Stirling University Heritage of Scotland Summer School. Later, Aonghas began writing the tunes down himself. He also has certain source books which he consults (see the *Related Collections* on p. 109), some of which he inherited from his uncle.

Using these written sources as a base, we turned to audio and video recordings to gain a fuller understanding of Aonghas' playing style. Aonghas has two solo commercial recordings available: *Highland Fiddle* (1977) and *The Hills of Glengarry* (2008); he has also contributed solo tracks to several other commercial recordings (see Discography, p. 109). Peggy provided audio-recordings of Aonghas' course at Stirling in July of 1984 and 1988, and David H. Arnold provided tapes of a week-long interview session in Lochyside in 2002. We also videotaped Aonghas playing and talking about the tunes on five occasions: in Arlington, Massachusetts in August 2003 and at Aonghas' home in Lochyside in September 2004, June 2005, December 2005 and May 2008.

All tunes labeled "Setting by Aonghas Grant" are transcriptions of Aonghas' playing. These transcriptions are drawn primarily from the videotaped performances; we also gathered information from the audio-recordings and from written sources. Our goal in the transcriptions was to present a version of each tune that was both readable and faithful to Aonghas' playing of that tune.

All performances on the DVD are from the 2003, 2004, 2005 and 2008 video recordings. Approximately half of the DVD tracks show the performance that we used when transcribing that tune.

Some tunes are presented without bowings or grace notes. The sources for these tunes are the handwritten music sheets that Aonghas uses when teaching or other printed collections.

Titles: Some tunes have several common names. We have included the main title(s) in the main title line. Alternate titles and English translations of Gaelic titles are included below in smaller type; the English translations are in quotes.

Text: Unless clearly marked as an editorial note, all text is by Aonghas. Some of it he wrote out himself, while other sections are transcribed from the video- and audio-recordings.

Variants: Aonghas frequently improvises melodic variants to the tunes. We've included a few such variants in smaller musical type below the tune (indicated by *1, *2). A transcription with no variants does not mean that Aonghas never varies that tune, but rather that we didn't have as many recorded sources to reference or that variants are already included in the tune. When there was a question about what was a variant and what was the tune, we asked Aonghas or referred to his handwritten versions of the tunes.

If a variant may be used in many similar places in the tune, it's often marked on just one or two of those spots. We haven't included variants that are easily inferred from the tune; for instance, in "My Gentle Milkmaid," Aonghas occasionally replaces bar three of the second part with bar one of the second part. In "Cabar Fèidh" (jig), the last four bars of the fourth part might be played like the last four bars of the second part.

Seconds: Aonghas often likes to have another fiddler play "seconds" (piping term used by Aonghas for a harmony part) in the slow airs and certain marches. He has collected a number of seconds over the years, including many composed by his students and colleagues.

Pipe Scale: Like many fiddlers, Aonghas adjusts certain notes when playing pipe tunes, as Highland bagpipes have their own particular scale and tuning: the C# on the pipes is slightly lower and the G♮ is slightly higher than on diatonic Western instruments. If the high G (on the E string) falls on a strong beat, Aonghas usually plays it as a G♮. If the high G is a passing tone on a weak beat, Aonghas sometimes plays it as a G#, depending on the scale and the context. These adjustments can happen within a single tune, and even within a single bar. Aonghas is usually very specific about whether a note is, for example, a G♮ or G#; occasionally he plays a note in between a G♮ and a G#. This "neutral" tone is very close to the actual pitch of the bagpipes' high G.

Sets: Aonghas often plays sets of two or more tunes. A very traditional listening or competition set for pipers and fiddlers is a march followed by a strathspey and a reel. These three tunes usually have the same tonic, or are in related keys. The march is almost invariably a four-part 2/4 pipe march. Aonghas plays the march once, with a very slight pause on the last cadence, and segues directly into the strathspey twice through and then into the reel. The reel is usually either a sixteen-bar tune played twice or a four-part pipe tune played once. Sometimes Aonghas pauses slightly between the strathspey and reel and at other times he goes straight from one to the other with no break.

Sets for dancing are usually a uniform set of tunes (e.g. all reels or all 6/8 pipe marches) in contrasting or alternating keys. Aonghas generally plays slow airs once or twice through as stand-alone pieces, but occasionally he follows a slow air with a jig or a strathspey and reel.

The tunes in this collection may be joined together in a variety of sets. On many pages, we have arranged the tunes so that they can be played together as a set if desired. Such sets are not specifically from Aonghas unless noted.

Mode: Aonghas has always centered his attention on the melody of his tunes and not on harmony or scale structure. Some of the tunes presented here are in straightforward major and minor keys, but much Highland repertoire is not possible to classify in this way, nor in the so-called "church modes" (e.g., Mixolydian, Dorian). For example, in pipe tunes, the relationship between melody and drone is more significant, and the neutral tones described above create a form of scale first described by Percy Grainger in terms of variable scale degrees: to force these into a classically-derived regularity is to miss some of the flavor or mood of these tunes. Some Scottish tunes are ambiguous about their tonal centre, and one of the best-known idioms in Scottish traditional music is the double-tonic, in which a melodic idea is repeated one step away and then returns to the starting pitch area.

Chords: Despite these modal ambiguities, many dance and concert musicians, both inside the Highlands and elsewhere, like to play these tunes with harmonic accompaniment. Chord progressions are very subjective, especially in pentatonic tunes and in pipe tunes. There are various possible approaches to accompaniment, and some Highland musicians use jazz-influenced harmonies to solve modal problems.

With each tune we have included chord progressions arranged by Barbara McOwen. The chords indicated here are relatively simple progressions in a modern Scottish dance band style. The reader may prefer to play without accompaniment or to improvise or write alternate chord progressions. Aonghas does not himself play any chordal instruments, though he often performs with accompaniment.

Key Signatures: The sharps and flats indicated at the beginning of each tune represent the notes needed to play that particular tune (and its corresponding grace notes and chords) with a minimum of accidentals, and do not necessarily correspond to the conventional definitions of keys. The annotation "on A," "on D," etc., indicates that the tune utilizes a scale starting on that pitch.

For Aonghas, the pitch level of certain tunes, especially slow airs, is not fixed. Sometimes Aonghas will play a tune one string up or down, sometimes one note up or down, and sometimes he'll add complexity and intensity to a slow air by changing it from a sharp key to a flat key, thus using fewer open strings and making more use of vibrato.

Aonghas remembers when Highland fiddlers tuned their violins below A-440, and he often prefers the sound of a tune played at a lower pitch.

Tempos: A metronome indication is given for most of the tunes based on Aonghas' performance of that tune in a recording. Although he is fairly consistent with the tempos of the marches and the dance tunes, the given tempos might vary a little in either direction according to dancing and performance needs.

We have included metronome indications for the slow airs as an aid to those unfamiliar with these tunes and their performance. Unlike the marches and dance tunes, which have a fairly small and predictable range of tempos, the slow airs as a group encompass a wide range of tempos. In addition, Aonghas very often pauses on certain notes within each phrase and at the end of the phrases. He is equally likely to let other parts tumble out at a much faster tempo than indicated. His emphasis on the pulse also varies widely: some airs have a completely horizontal flow with no discernible beat at all while others have quite a strong beat, or a section with a stronger beat. Thus, for the slow airs learners might like to use a metronome to get the feel for the tempo but then turn the metronome off!

BOWING

Aonghas holds his bow conventionally at the frog with a strong yet relaxed grip. He is typical of many Highland fiddle players in that his bowings are improvised and he is often unaware of his exact bowings as he plays. He characterizes himself as an "up-bow player" and frequently uses up-bows on the downbeats.

Creative variation in bowing is an important part of Aonghas' style, and he varies his bowing considerably from one day to the next, and even from one moment to the next. The bowings printed here, therefore, are representative of Aonghas' style but may be interpreted in a number of ways: they may be played exactly, ignored completely or glanced at occasionally, perhaps after the notes of the tune are learned. Improvised grace-notes and improvised variants of the melody notes often affect the bowing, particularly if they engender different string crossings or change the number of notes in a figure.

Two-note slurring on reels: Aonghas often slurs the eighth notes (quavers) of a reel in pairs, with an up-bow at the beginning of each bar. His bow arm pulses each note and subtly subdivides the eighths (quavers) into sixteenths (semiquavers), making this a very driving and exciting bowing pattern. According to Aonghas, this bowing "seems to be a Highland style. You always heard the old boys play like that."

Lilt and swing on reels and jigs: Lilt or swing – the subtle varying of note lengths – is an essential component of Aonghas' fiddling and no standard notation can capture the rhythmic intricacies of his playing. Eighth notes (quavers) in reels, for instance, are played somewhere between

 and

Likewise, eighth notes (quavers) in jigs are played somewhere between

 and

We have chosen to notate certain reels and jigs as "dotted" and others as "straight" but in actuality they all fall somewhere between these two extremes.

Snaps in reels: Aonghas often plays snaps in reels:

and sometimes he plays a snap on three distinct notes:

Birls: Aonghas always plays birls on the down-bow, with a rapid, energetic quiver in his bow arm. He tends to place birls on the second beat.

Strathspey bowings: Aonghas' overall sound is legato, with fairly long bows but a "bite" at each bow change. However, in strathspeys Aonghas often dramatically lifts the bow. For instance,

is performed like this

Certain particularly complex bowings are indicated in greater detail in the transcriptions.

Hooked bows: A slur with long lines over or under the notes indicates a slight stopping of the bow between notes. This is not a short or percussive effect, but rather a gentle re-articulation. Aonghas generally uses this technique in slower tunes.

FINGERING TECHNIQUE

Aonghas' right hand is his fingering hand and he bows left-handed, or "corrie-fisted." Aonghas never had any formal training, but holds the fiddle much like classical violinists do: a fairly straight right wrist, right elbow movement in string changes, slightly rounded relaxed fingers over the strings and a relaxed thumb. He teaches finger patterns for different scales and uses vibrato and higher positions. Aonghas rarely uses the fourth finger unless for the high B and for grace notes. The brilliance of the open strings and the "bite" of the bow in string changes are a significant part of his playing style.

Grace-notes: In keeping with standard piping notation, we have written all grace-notes as thirty-second notes (demisemiquavers). Some of these are "crushed" (almost simultaneous with the decorated note) and others are "melodic" (played slower and with each note distinct). Most grace-notes are slurred to the following melody note, although occasionally Aonghas slurs a grace-note to the preceding melody note.

This grace-note is often called a "flick" or an "upper mordent;" Aonghas sometimes calls it a "stot." It is done extremely quickly and the resulting effect is more percussive than melodic.

Occasionally, Aonghas strings two flicks together.

Sometimes Aonghas precedes a flick with another grace-note, in effect "gracing the grace-note." In this case, the stems of the two grace-notes are not connected:

One of the hallmarks of Aonghas' style is the simultaneous playing of a flick with the fingering hand and a snap with the bow arm. Aonghas primarily uses this effect in reels and occasionally in strathspeys. This "flick plus snap" usually replaces a quarter note (crotchet) in the melody, but sometimes the flick is added to an existing snap. It is always played down-up and the resulting effect can sound similar to a birl.

A grace-note with a diamond-shaped notehead indicates that Aonghas rolls his hand and fingers from back to front slightly while playing both the grace note and the following melody note. Although his fingers do not actually slide on the string, the resulting sound is that of a small slide.

Trills and turns: The "running trill" is the only grace-note for which Aonghas has a name and it is always a second-finger trill on a first-finger melody note. The second finger starts close to the first finger and then "runs" up the fingerboard, flattening and straightening as it goes. The trill may start on either the upper or lower note and the number of iterations of the trill varies: usually two, sometimes three. Says Aonghas, "You start down here and work your way up."

In certain slow tunes, Aonghas plays a "classical-style" trill or turn. All the notes are played clearly and distinctly.

Turn: notated:  played:

Double-stops: Double-stops are written with two note-head sizes. The larger one is the melody note.

Some double-stops have small diamond-shaped noteheads. This means that Aonghas touches the double-stopping note quickly but doesn't sustain it for the duration of the melody note.

Slides: Up and down slides are indicated like this:

Note that this example also includes fingering. In general, fingerings are marked only when Aonghas shifts positions.

A tune in Aonghas' own handwriting

Aonghas Grant, Caol, Lochaber, 2004

Aonghas Grant, Highland Fiddler

By Peggy Duesenberry and Laura Risk

Aonghas Grant is widely recognized as one of the most important living exponents of Scottish Highland fiddling, a style that has been significantly influenced by the associated traditions of Gaelic song and Highland piping. Born in 1931, Aonghas was raised in the West Highlands: his father's family had lived in the Glengarry region for generations. In addition to this legacy of Highland tradition, Aonghas has also been involved in many of the significant changes and trends in Scottish traditional music during his lifetime, and he is always keen to learn new tunes from many sources. This collection reflects both older and newer aspects of his musical life, with a focus on repertoire he especially associates with the Highlands.

Aonghas plays left-handed: when playing fiddle, he fingers with his right hand and bows with his left. When playing the pipes, his right hand is on top and his left hand is on the bottom. He has reversed the strings on his violin (from left to right, they are E A D G instead of G D A E) and, to an observer, his playing is the mirror image of a conventional right-handed fiddler.

EARLY INFLUENCES

Aonghas grew up in a musical family, amongst much community music-making, and his most important musical influence was his paternal uncle, Archie Grant. Says Aonghas, "When I knew him first, he was an old man and he stayed away up in the back of beyond." Uncle Archie gave Aonghas instruments, showed him basic playing techniques and was an important source of repertoire. Other early influences included his father, who played the clarsach and some fiddle but was best known as a Gaelic singer. "My father was a bit of a bard," recalls Aonghas. "When he died in 1943, five hundred years of stories and songs were lost with him." His uncle Allan was a good fiddler but died before Aonghas was born.

Aonghas' first instrument was the Highland bagpipes, which he began to play at the age of 7 or 8. "We had one of my Uncle Archie's chanters in the house and he'd come up and he'd play. It was him that started me learning the chanter." Like many other Highland fiddlers of his generation, Aonghas took up the fiddle as a second instrument in his teens. He began playing the fiddle at age 13: "When I got the fiddle from my uncle and he was showing me how to finger and bow the notes, and within half an hour I could play "Dornoch Links" [2/4 pipe march, see Vol. 2] and within a couple of days I could play practically everything I could play on the chanter... Instinctively you knew where to put your fingers."

Local musicians influenced Aonghas as well. "There were droves of old fiddlers around that were all born in the 1800s and still on the go then in the 1930s and '40s," he says, recalling that many of the older fiddlers held their fiddles down "in the crook of their arm." Uncle Archie held his fiddle up on his shoulder, but with his chin on the E-string side of the tailpiece, and this is how Aonghas holds his fiddle, too.

Aonghas recalls his Uncle Archie and other older fiddlers in Glengarry using double-stops, and has theorized that these double-stops may have developed out of the old bardic harp tradition: "You see, Allan Dall MacDougal, the last harper, used to come down, he was also a great fiddler and so was his son, a great fiddler. So they probably had a lot of influence. This is why, all over Glengarry and that area, fiddlers used a lot of double-stops. Because when I came down to Inverailort, the MacRae boys had never heard double-stops. Didn't know what I was doing, putting them in the Gaelic airs and that. Now I realize that probably Allan Dall with his knowledge of harmony on the harp, would be doing double-stops quite naturally on the fiddle in airs and things."

Aonghas finished school at fourteen and began working as a ghillie. Soon he was hired as a shepherd in Culachy, just south of Fort Augustus, and by the age of twenty, he was the best sheep-shearer on the estate. He continued to play fiddle, visiting his uncle Archie occasionally and making frequent trips to the home of Jock and Chrissy Kirkpatrick. Jock, the sheep manager on the nearby Ardachy estate, played fiddle and melodeon, and Chrissy played piano. Unlike Aonghas and Jock, Chrissy could read music. Aonghas recalls many "friendly Saturday nights... playing fiddle tunes for hours," particularly in the winter when work was slow.

PLAYING FOR DANCES

When he was fourteen, Aonghas began going to the local dances in Fort Augustus, Invergarry, Invermoriston and Glenurquhart. The band was usually made up of local musicians including Jock Kirkpatrick and fiddler Peter MacDonald, who was also a Gaelic singer. A few years later Peter MacDonald and Archie MacNaughton, who played the two-row accordion, invited Aonghas to play with them regularly for local dances. Although pre-war bands in the Highlands usually included a few fiddles, piano and drums, accordions became more common after the war.

In the mid-1950s Aonghas moved to Inverailort Estate, west of Fort William, and worked as a shepherd and deer-stalker. The Manager of the estate was Farquhar MacRae, who played fiddle and the button-key accordion. Aonghas had never met Farquhar before, but they shared a common Highland repertoire. Aonghas did notice, however, that the fiddle style around Inverailort was slightly different from the Glengarry style.

Farquhar invited Aonghas to join his band, the Roshven Ceilidh Band, which also included a drummer and occasionally a second accordion player. The band played dances throughout the Highlands, covering a radius of nearly 100 miles. At the time, recalls Aonghas, dances were "the only big social event. Most Fridays there was a dance, and sometimes even on a Wednesday there'd be a wee hop, and sometimes on Saturday night." The dances included Eightsome reels, Dundee Reel, Petronella, Dashing White Sergeant, Strip the Willow, lancers, quadrilles, and couple dances such as Highland Schottische, Canadian Barn Dance, Seven-Step Polka, Boston Two-Step, Military Two-Step, Eva Three-Step and waltzes.

Says Aonghas, "When Farquhar's band was playing, people came from miles, everywhere, because he was so great for dancing. He had an excellent, first-class tempo for dancing." The band never played concerts, always dances or weddings, and each musician earned two or three pounds per night.

The atmosphere on the bandstand was casual and relaxed. "The MC would say, 'Strip the Willow,' and Farquhar would just say, 'Pipe jigs, boys,' and away, and the second time, you know, 'Irish jigs'... We would very seldom say what tune we were about to play. We'd played together so much, all us boys, we just, from the first note, knew. Compared to the South country boys, with music stuck in front of them! ...We never ever practiced or anything. We just came in and played. I could be at a sheep-shearing until eight o'clock at night and have a quick splash and away down and play at a dance."

It was while playing for a dance that Aonghas met his future wife, Moira MacLeod, and they were married a few years later. They moved to Glenfinnan and Aonghas continued to play in Farquhar's band, as well as with Fergie MacDonald and others in the region.

Around 1965, Aonghas and Moira moved to Caol, just outside Fort William. Aonghas had taken a job with the Forestry Commission, skippering a boat that was transporting culvert pipes and other building equipment to road crews. Aonghas later joined the road crew himself and spent many years building roads throughout the Highlands.

He continued to play with Farquhar's band very occasionally, although "there was a period there when I was working that I was hardly playing at all."

SOLO FIDDLE PLAYING

In the late 1950s, Aonghas became more interested in slow airs, partly as a result of hearing Kreisler pieces on the radio. He was enthralled by the warmth of tone and feeling, along with the double-stop playing of classical violinists. After manfully trying to learn "Liebeslied" from a Kreisler recording, he realized that the singing tone could also be used in the Gaelic song repertoire he already knew and soon gained a reputation for his beautiful slow air playing. Listening to radio and 78 rpm records had further influences: at the age of 26 or 27, he attempted flat keys for the first time, inspired by hearing Hector MacAndrew in radio broadcasts. Likewise, he worked out shifting positions through listening to a recording of Mackenzie Murdoch playing "Auld Robin Gray;" he then started to use shifting when playing Gaelic airs for waltzes. Both flat keys and shifting were rare among Highland fiddlers at that time.

In 1969, Aonghas entered the Blairgowrie fiddle competition with a set of "Niel Gow's Lament for the Death of his Second Wife," "J.F. MacKenzie" (strathspey), and "Captain MacDiarmid" (reel). Aonghas was the last of 31 competitors to play. The well-known Shetland folklorist and fiddler Tom Anderson was judging and he immediately awarded first prize to Aonghas, saying, "I can hear the pipe chanter coming through." Around this time, Aonghas also won the National Mod Competition three times in a row, and he was recorded by the School of Scottish Studies in 1969 and 1970 for its sound archive. This connection led to further invitations, including recording the award-winning LP *Highland Fiddle* for Topic Records. Aonghas performed at the 1976 Smithsonian Bicentennial celebrations in Washington, D.C. and has played in Norway, Denmark, Holland, France, Brittany and Ireland.

TEACHING

In Aonghas' young days, formal fiddle teaching was unknown in the Highlands. His own informal learning was more typical, and he had never thought to give lessons or classes himself until Tom Anderson invited him to teach at the University of Stirling Heritage of Scotland Summer School in 1979. In over 20 years of teaching at this two-week residential course, Aonghas enjoyed meeting a variety of musicians and hearing their tunes, and he learned much more about written music. Aonghas has also taught at various summer schools in North America. Closer to home, he has been involved in the highly successful Fèisean movement and currently teaches private students at his home in Lochyside. In 1996, he began teaching undergraduate fiddle students at the Royal Scottish Academy of Music and Drama in Glasgow, starting with Allan Henderson, Iain MacFarlane and Sharon Hassan. Aonghas' work as a teacher, along with his own playing, has made an important contribution to the flourishing Highland music scene today.

Photographs & Illustrations

Original artwork by Evelyn Turner, 2008, on pages vi, xiii, xvii, 8, 10, 22, 34, 35, 41,
57, 59, 62, 64, 65, 79, 94, 95, 110, 113, 115, 116
All photographs and artwork are copyright and used with permission

Slow Tunes

Memories of Ardachy

Slow Air on D

By Aonghas Grant
Setting by Aonghas Grant

(𝅗𝅥. = 32)

Seconds—Memories of Ardachy

Seconds by Barbara McOwen

To Chrissie, with love from Aonghas, February 7, 1995.

This tune was composed for my oldest friend, Chrissie Kirkpatrick, for her 90th birthday. Her husband was Jock Kirkpatrick (see "Jock's Fiddle," p. 104). They were a great influence on me. There would be a big session for hours on a Saturday night at their house up in the hills in Tom a' Mhòid. She could play piano and took lessons and could read music a bit, and she was a big help in learning the tunes. Neither Jock nor myself could read the music. I remember one time we were playing through a set; she said, "What do you want me to do?" "Oh just vamp like hell," he says.

She died at age 97 and I played this air in the kirk at her funeral, on Jock's fiddle.

Fiona and Gavin's Wedding

Waltz on F

(♩ = 40)

By Aonghas Grant
Setting by Aonghas Grant

Fiona MacLeod was a student of mine; I've known her all her life. She is a singer, too. In 2004 she married Gavin Thornley. The original transcription was by Val Bryan.

Cairena's Air

Slow Air on Eb

(♩ = 44)

By Aonghas Grant

Composed for Cairena Campbell, a pupil at Stirling University and a good friend, and notated by John Marshall, Portree, September 2003. Cairena's a fine fiddler and won the Mòd a few years ago.

Farquhar's Waltz
Waltz on D

(♩ = 132)

By Farquhar MacRae (1925–2000)
Setting by Aonghas Grant

quick waltz

[Reproduced by permission of Hetty MacRae]

"Farquhar's Waltz" (the Gaelic spelling is "Fearchar") was composed by Farquhar MacRae. It's one of the few tunes he made, round about 1954. After he married Hetty it became known as "Farquhar and Hetty's Waltz." We worked together on the Inverailort Estate when he was also a shepherd, and eventually Manager. He was a renowned musician, both on the fiddle and the button-key box. He was an expert in playing pipe reels and jigs, and his band was the Roshven Ceilidh Band, which was famous throughout the West Coast. Hundreds of people came to his funeral in Glenfinnan. Before the service, eight fiddlers and two box players played Gaelic airs in the choir loft, and we played this tune—slowed down a bit—as they carried his coffin out of the church.

The Roshven Ceilidh Band, Morar Hotel in Morar, 1958
Simon MacKinnon (piano box), Georgie Howie (drums), Aonghas, Farquhar MacRae (button box)

Cille Choirill

"Cyril's Cell"
Slow Air on C   (𝅗𝅥. = 44)

By Kenneth Kennedy (1919–1996)
Setting by Aonghas Grant

Kenny Kennedy was a native of Brae Lochaber. His father, Jock Kennedy, was head Keeper in Glen Roy and was a very fine fiddler. Kenny was for many years a sheep farmer at Brunachan in Glen Roy. We used to buy rams from him. Kenny was an excellent player on the mouth organ and composed a number of tunes. This is his best known one.

Cille Choirill is an old burial ground still in use. My grandmother's people, the Stewarts, have been buried there since the early 1700s. There is a chapel there which has been restored in recent years with help from people from Cape Breton whose ancestors worshipped there. A few times a year they still hold a Gaelic Mass in the Chapel. Kenny's sister, Ann MacDonnell, was a famous local historian. Sadly both are now at rest in Cille Choirill. It's a beautiful spot, it's away up at the brim of the hill. I'd like to be planted there myself. It's called in Gaelic "the knoll of the angels." The same people are buried in the same parts for generations. This poem is by Kenny Kennedy:

O' where in the whole world, such beauty and peace,
As Cille Choirill, in the Braes of Lochaber,
'Neath the green mossy mounds, many Clans lie asleep,
All around, are the hills they did wander.

In this Heavn' on Earth, rest ancestors blest,
Their children so true, shall never forget,
Till the hills fade away, and the last tune is played,
With love, they will always remember.

Heather Manson's Wedding Waltz

Waltz on D   (𝅘𝅥 = 116)

By Aonghas Grant
Setting by Aonghas Grant

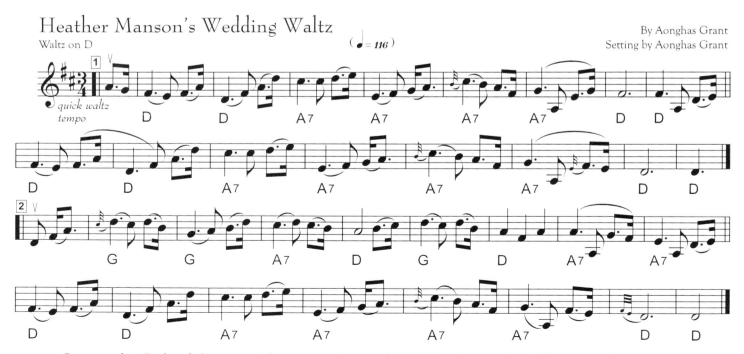

Composed in Barbara's house in Arlington, in August of 2003. Heather is a fine fiddle pupil of mine.

Tam's Old Love Song
Slow Air on D   (♩ = 76)   As played by Aonghas Grant

Seconds—Tam's Old Love Song
Seconds by Wattie Robson

[Reproduced by permission of Springthyme Music]

This was first written out by Pete Shepheard from the playing of Tam Hughes and Wattie Robson. Peter is an English guy who started up the TMSA (Traditional Music and Song Association of Scotland), and also Springthyme Records, in Fife. Tam was a famous Borders fiddler, who worked on farms around Jedburgh all his life. He had a record out—*Tam Hughes, Border Fiddler*. This is a tune which Tam learned from his family, but he never knew the name of it, so everyone called it "Tam's Old Love Song."

Aonghas working on *The Glengarry Collection*, February 2002, Lochyside

Mairi Nighean Dheòrsa

"Mairi, daughter of George" ❖ Grant of Sheuglie's contest betwixt his Violin, Pipe and Harp
Slow Air on A

(♩ = 40)   Setting by Aonghas Grant

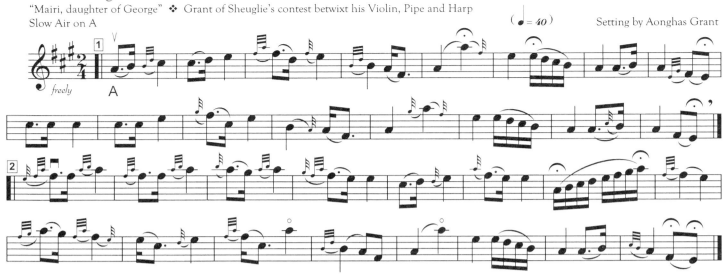

Sheuglie is up in Glenurquhart. You can hear the three different instruments in the music—some pibroch variations, harp runs, and violin harmonics. This is from the *Knockie Collection*. My uncle used to play it, but he put it in a different key, I think it was lower down.

Mrs. Forsyth's Pibroch ❖ Manse of Abernethy

Slow Air on A

By Charles Grant (1806–1892)

One of my pupils, Charlotte Moodie from America, who married the son of a good friend of ours, played this for me in a lesson and she did a very good job of it. Charles Grant was born in Strondhu, Strathspey and was Headmaster at Aberlour. He was a violin pupil of William Marshall, and inherited Marshall's violin.

Greig's Strathspey

Slow Air on Bb or G   (♩ = 60)   Setting by Aonghas Grant

A favourite tune of Niel Gow. It's usually played as an air.

The Grant B&B, Caol, Lochyside, Inverness-shire, 2004

Fuadach Nan Gaidheal

Lord Lovat's Lament ❖ "Lament for the Highland Clearances"
Lament on F

(♩ = 44)

Setting by Aonghas Grant

with a gentle pulse

Seconds—Fuadach Nan Gaidheal

Seconds by Donald Riddell (1908-1992)

A well-known Gaelic song air, a lament for the Highland Clearances. This is one of the verses in English translation:

> I mourn for the Highlands, so dear and forsaken,
> Land of the Clansmen so gallant and brave,
> To make way for sportsmen their lands were all taken,
> And they had to seek new homes far over the wave.

There were many Lord Lovats over the centuries, the family name being Fraser. The Lord Lovat at the time of the Boer War raised the regiment known as the Lovat Scouts, composed of the Highland deerstalkers and shepherds, mostly all crack shots.

Killiecrankie

Slow March on C   (♩ = 60)   Setting by Aonghas Grant

It's a stunning tune, a slow-ish march, not unlike the style the Cape Breton boys play. There are two or three tunes about Killiecrankie. This one is from the *Inverness Collection*; in some collections it's put as an air. *[It appears in the key of D in O'Neill's 1001 Gems as "Planxty Davis."—Ed.]*

The actual battle is called *The Battle of George's Field*, in 1689. General MacKay's army was down below, he was fighting the charge uphill. The Highlanders with James Graham—Bonnie Dundee as he was called—were up on high ground, and apparently the sun was in their eyes, so they waited all day til about 7 when the sun dipped below the hill, then they charged down. It was all over in a few minutes. But Dundee was killed that day. He had worn a green doublet, and all the Highlanders were horrified, as it was said this would offend the fairy-folk. Here just on the point of victory he took a musket-ball. It changed the whole course of Scottish history. He was a great general, and if he hadn't got killed, he would have swept the Stewarts back in then, in the 1600s. That was the first Jacobite Rising, where they were trying to get King James, Prince Charlie's father, back—the Old Pretender. But once Dundee got killed, it petered out. They'd nobody to take over, and that was it, they all dispersed.

The Queen's View, 1991: Loch Tummel, Killiecrankie nearby,
Mt Schiehallion in the distance on the left

Archibald MacDonnell of Keppoch

Lament on D (♩. = 34)

Setting by Aonghas Grant

Seconds—Archibald MacDonnell of Keppoch

Seconds by Meg Magower

Keppoch's just up the road here. It's actually MacDonnell (pron. mac-don-ELL). The best man at my wedding was Angus MacDonnell, of old Glengarry stock, and my father was related to the MacDonnells too. Archie of the famous tune was the Chief of the MacDonnells of Keppoch. He went to Culloden. They made an awful mess of things apart from picking Culloden for a battle in the first place. The MacDonnells always fought at the right-hand side of the King, and here they had them all mixed up, and they were annoyed at this. The English had cannon and were firing grape shot, the Highlanders just stood there like idiots, not knowing what was happening, and they were getting mowed down by the grape shot. They couldn't take shelter anywhere on the field. Finally Keppoch got fed up, took off and led the charge. They got all bogged down and he got killed. There were a thousand of them killed, just in the matter of half an hour.

The brother of this guy went out to Jamaica after the 1745-46 rebellion. He and his wife both died there. The one daughter came back and she was brought up by her two uncles at Keppoch, and it was her that married into some relation on my mother's side.

I taught this one of the early years at Stirling University, and Meg Magower did the Seconds part. Meg was just a young kid at the time, about 15. There were two other two girls, Rosemary Stewart, and Rhiannon Jenkins, and all three of them had fathers who were teachers at the University, and both Rhiannon and Rosemary became doctors— Rosemary is now living in Boulder, Colorado.

Niel Gow's Farewell to Whisky

Lament on G

(♩ = 52)

By Niel Gow (1727–1807)
Setting by Aonghas Grant

There are two stories about this. Some say Niel was on the drams and fell on top of his fiddle coming out of Staredam one night in the wintertime. He was carrying it, his Italian fiddle which he got from Murray of Abercairney, in a green velvet bag, and slipped on ice, fell on top of it, and cracked it down the front. When he woke up the next morning and realized he'd cracked his fiddle, he was full of remorse for what he'd done and went on the tack for three months, which is a record for any fiddler, and composed "Niel Gow's Farewell to Whisky." Then he went up to play at the Caledonian Northern Ball in Inverness. There was a big bowl of punch for the band on the stage, sort of behind the curtains, with glasses and a big toddy ladle. Every two or three dances all these boys from the band would go in and fill their glasses. It got too much for Niel and he eventually joined them and broke the tack and composed a rousing "Whisky welcome back again." And I don't think he ever went on the tack again—he stayed on the drams after that.

The other story is that there were a couple of years of bad harvest. Barley and oats were scarce, and were needed to feed the animals and the people, barley particularly, so they weren't using it to make whisky, which caused a low production of whisky.

For some odd reason over the centuries, this tune has changed—it's very seldom played as a slow air, it's played as a reel.

Niel Gow's Other Fiddle—not the Gasparo da Salo—Blair Castle, 1992

Forneth House

Slow Air on D   (♩ = 48)

By Robert Petrie (1767–1830)
Setting by Aonghas Grant

Seconds—Forneth House

Seconds by Bill Cook

Forneth House is in Perthshire, not far from Dunkeld. Robert Petrie was a gardener to trade, working for big house gardens such as Forneth. Robert Petrie was also a famous fiddler in Perthshire, a contemporary of the Gows, and was perhaps a bit overshadowed by Gow. He composed some very good tunes and published a collection. When Sir Walter Scott organized King George's visit to Edinburgh, as part of the celebrations the City Fathers held a fiddle competition which was judged by Nathaniel Gow from behind a screen (this is still done in some competitions in Scotland). Petrie won, the prize was a silver mounted bow. The other fiddlers complained, saying Petrie knew Gow because he lived near Dunkeld. The competition was held again the next day. The fiddlers had to play new tunes. Petrie won again and that was the end of the matter.

This is almost more of a Slow Strathspey. A Slow Strathspey would have a bit more bite than an air. But not too slow—it's 4/4.

Mrs Hamilton of Pencaitland

Slow Air on C

By Nathaniel Gow (1763–1831)
Setting by Aonghas Grant

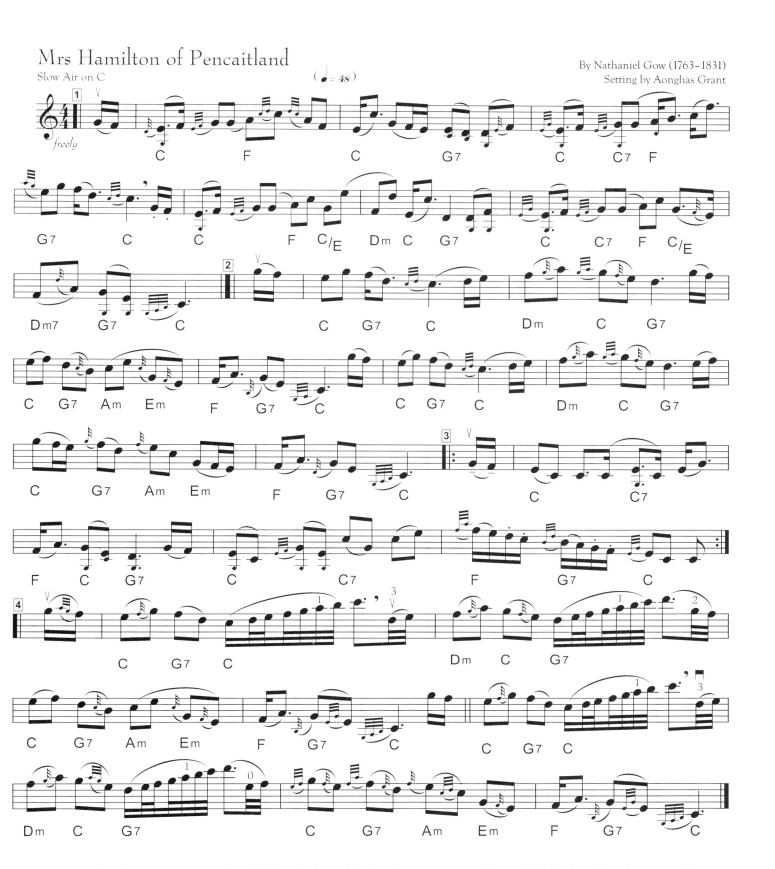

Pencaitland is an estate outside Edinburgh. I usually play this as a set together with "North of the Grampians" and "The Haggis." They're all in C. I won the Northern Counties Fiddle Championship in Inverness many years ago with this set.

Tuireadh Iain Ruaidh

"Iain Ruaidh's Lament"
Gaelic Song Air on D

(♩.= 32)

By Edward Pursell (1891–1964)
Setting by Aonghas Grant

I also play this in Bb. Edward Pursell wrote the music and the words. He was the headmaster in the school districts on the Kintyre peninsula. He taught himself the Gaelic language and won the Aberdeen Mod in 1939 for his poem "Moladh Màiri." The tune sounds like it could be the ground of an old pibroch.

[Edward Pursell was awarded the gold medal in the Literary Section of the National Mod and twice won the Cassilis Cup for Literature, the second time in 1946. That same year he was crowned Bard, thus gaining the highest honor of the Mod. Mr. Pursell was headmaster of Tighnabruaich School from 1923 to 1932 and of Kinloch School in Campbeltown from 1932 until 1956.–Ed.]

Nighean Donn a' Chuailein Rìomaich

"Maid with the flowing tresses"
Gaelic Song Air on D

(♩.= 52)

Setting by Aonghas Grant

I play this in two or three different keys. It's in D or G for the students but I usually play it in F. I recently played it as a waltz for a wedding.

Mo Mhàthair

"My Mother"
Gaelic Song Air on Bb

By Neil MacLean (20th cent.)
Setting by Aonghas Grant

Everybody else plays this in D, but I play it in Bb. Neil MacLean composed it—he's a famous bard, known as the Govan Bard. He was from Mull originally, but stayed in Govan, outside Glasgow. I first heard this after the war. Calum Kennedy used to do a beautiful job of singing it. Renwick MacArthur wrote it down from my playing the first year at Stirling University. A lot of people play these Gaelic airs in waltz time, but they're really not that—they're more pointed.

Creag Ghuanach

"The Tottering Rock"
Gaelic Song Air on G

Setting by Aonghas Grant

The tottering rock is a sheltering rock on the hills above Loch Treig. The first part is the Sèisd (chorus) and the second part is the Rann (verse). It's part of a big long story from the point of view of the wise owl. It's a Lochaber song, composed by the bard Donald McKillop, known as Donald Finlay of the Songs. He composed a lot of songs and poems about nature. He lived in Strathossian, Corrour in the 1600s, and is buried in Cille Choirill in Lochaber. Much later the tune was used for the song "Mingulay Boat Song."

Cha Tig Mòr mo Bhean Dhachaigh

Lochaber No More
Gaelic Song Air on G

(♩ = 48)

Setting by Aonghas Grant

This is the original source of the tune in Lochaber. There are modern words by James Hogg.

The tune is known in English as "Lochaber No More," but the translation of the Gaelic is "Marion my wife will never return." The words are supposed to be this man telling his little daughter that her mother will never be coming back, because she's dying. Very sad. It's usually played on the pipes at funerals, usually walking along when the coffin is being carried to the grave. There's not a dry eye when it's played. At one time somebody said it was banned from being played in the Highland regiments because it would unman the men—they used to weep openly at it, because they've got so many sad things in the Highlands. Also the Irish claim to have a version of it from Limerick. When the Irish surrendered at the Siege of Limerick, they were forced into conditions that would make them leave the island forever. They were put on a sailing boat and taken away, with the wives and children weeping at the loch side. That's a sad thing too. The Irish call it "Lament for Limerick"—it's the same tune, though played a bit differently.

Muinntir a' Ghlinne Seo

Lament for Glencoe Massacre
Gaelic Song Air on Bb

(♩. = 40)

Setting by Aonghas Grant

"Lament for Glencoe Massacre" is very similar to a tune called "Lord Breadalbane's March." Ironic, because the Breadalbanes were associated with the Campbells, who were responsible for the massacre. The *Inverness Collection* calls it "Mhnathan a' Ghlinne Seo"—"Women of the Glen." "Played by a piper to warn the sleeping MacDonalds on the morning of the Massacre of Glencoe."

My Uncle Archie used to play it in Eb, on the back strings.

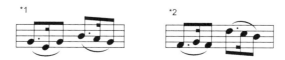

Gleann Bhaile Chaoil

"Ballachulish Glen"
Gaelic Song Air on D

By John Cameron (active 1850s)
Setting by Aonghas Grant

Seconds—Gleann Bhaile Chaoil

The music and the words are by John Cameron, a famous bard from Glencoe. He was a Ballachulish man but served as a policeman for many years in Paisley. He also wrote "Mist Covered Mountains." This one's a song about the beauty of the Glen, from the point of view of someone far away.

Loch Leven and Ballachulish Bridge, from the Village of Glencoe

Cumha Chailean Ghlinn-Iubhar le Cho-dhalta

"A Lament for Campbell of Glenure"
Gaelic Song Air on C

(ϕ. = 30)

Setting by Aonghas Grant

It's been over two hundred years since he was shot, Colin Campbell of Glenure, in the Wood of Lettermore, on the 8th of November, 1752. James Stewart of Acharn Appin, Seumas a' Ghlinne as he was called, James of the Glen, was hung for it although innocent. Allan Breck was a cousin of the Stewart chief, who was in exile in France, and he and James were looking after the interests of the Stewarts in the glen, which was being taken over by the Campbells. Campbell had worked his way through most of the upper glen, taken over farms, kicked out the tenants, and he was collecting taxes. One day he came up the wood in the moor, and he was shot in the back right off the horse. James Stewart was working at the farm, he wasn't near the place at all. But he was taken out to Inveraray and jailed. There was a trial, there were twelve Campbells on the jury, and he was found guilty. He was taken up to the end of Ballachulish Bridge, called Cnap a' Chaolais, and hung there. The Campbells were so vindictive, that when he was hung, they chained his body together and he was there for two and a half years. Even when it started falling apart, they wired it up again. There were four redcoats guarding him. Eventually some of the Stewarts got the guards drunk, cut the body down, wrapped it in a sailcloth, into a boat, down into the sea, below Ballachulish Bridge, and buried him on this little island off Appin. When the heat died down, some years later, they gathered up his bones, and buried him in old Keil Cemetery. Back in the 20s or 30s, one of his relations, Col. Stewart of Appin, put up a plaque, "Here lies Seumas of the Glen, hung for the murder of Colin Campbell, a crime of which he was totally innocent." It's amazing—to this day the secret of the murderer has been handed down through the generations and is known to only one family.

One of the sad things about it was himself and Campbell were of equal social standing, and they were fairly friendly, they used to have a drink or two together, and a few days before the murder they met in the Inn at Appin. There was a bit of a fallout because some of the Appin crowd were going to get shifted out of the farm and some of the Campbells were going to get shifted in. But Campbell apparently had been invited the next evening to James Stewart's house for a meal and when he came there James Stewart, always the gentleman, apologized for the night before, and they were all okay. But some of the Campbells had seen the fallout at the Inn, so they put the blame on poor James Stewart.

Some years ago there appeared a cairn with a plaque on it at the spot where Campbell was shot. There were some boulders way up behind it, and you could see where somebody had shifted some of the stones, and it was an ideal place to lie down with a long musket, through this gap, and get him as he came through a wee bit of a gully— it's an ideal ambush place. One theory was this young MacDonnell of Keppoch was supposed to be the best shot in Lochaber, he was the hitman. And then there was one of the Stewarts of Ballachulish—apparently on the day of the hanging he was wanting to rush out of the house, and some of the rest held him down, and other people think it was actually him that did it. There was nobody who actually came forward to say at the eleventh hour that "It was me that did it, not James." That was sad.

This tune was composed for Campbell by his foster brother, and Robert Louis Stevenson incorporated part of the story into *Kidnapped*. He called Colin Campbell the "Red Fox"—he was called Cailean Ruadh in Gaelic, Red Colin, but he was never actually called the Red Fox.

Criogal Cridhe

"Gregor My Love"
Gaelic Song Air on G   (♩ = *32*)   Setting by Aonghas Grant

Said to be composed by the wife of Gregor MacGregor. He was hanged by the Campbells down at Taymouth Castle, Loch Tayside, in 1570. One of the famous singers of this song said that this is *the* most evocative of all the Gaelic songs. I play this in various keys—F is also good.

"Clan Stewart of Appin" at Culloden

Cearcall a' Chuain

"The Circle of the Ocean"   By Calum and Rory MacDonald
Gaelic Song Air on D   (♩. = *44*)   Setting by Aonghas Grant

Calum and Rory MacDonald are brothers in the band Runrig. This is a modern Gaelic song which has become one of the "classics." *[Reproduced by permission of the copyright holders, C&R MacDonald, Storr Music]*

Òran Mòr MhicLeòid

In Praise of the Chief ❖ "Big Song of the MacLeods"
Gaelic Song Air on D

1 (♩. = 46)   2 (♩. = 54)

Setting by Aonghas Grant

This is one of two songs praising Iain Breac MacLeòid, or Speckled John (1646-1713). He was the very popular and greatly admired Clan Chief of the MacLeods. He kept a harper, a piper, a bard and a fool in his residence at Dunvegan Castle, and treated the artists with respect. After Iain died he was succeeded by his son Ruairidh Òg, who was not the great chief that Iain was. The words to this song were written by the harper, Ruaraidh Dall Morison, and it praises the virtues of the former Chief in great contrast to his successor. "Dall" means "blind"—he was blinded by smallpox, as was the great Irish harper Turlough O' Carolan.

Dunvegan Castle, Isle of Skye, the seat of Clan MacLeod

Sìne Bhàn

"Fair Jean"
Gaelic Song Air on D

(𝅗𝅥. = 46)

Setting by Aonghas Grant

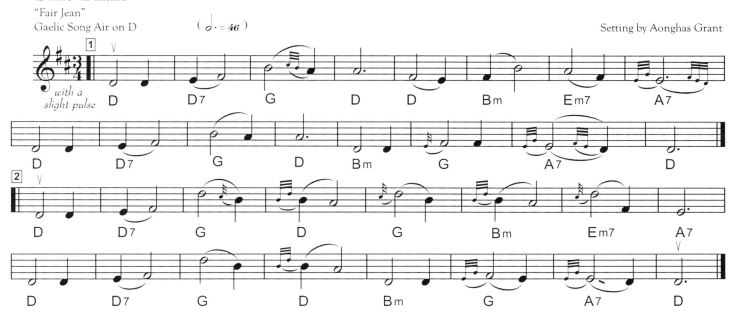

Duncan Johnston was born on Islay. He wrote the words of this song when he went away to the First World War. He came through the war without a scratch, and when he came back, he got married to his sweetheart. It's my very favourite Gaelic song—one of the only ones with a happy ending.

He'n Clò-dubh

"This is the black cloth" ❖ In Praise of the Tartan
Gaelic Song Air on G

(𝅗𝅥 = 72)

By Alasdair MacDonald of Moidart (ca. 1695 – ca. 1770)
Setting by Aonghas Grant

Seconds—He'n Clò-dubh

Seconds by Barbara McOwen

It's a song about the black cloth, but "I prefer the tartan." Alasdair MacDonald was the famous Moidart bard of the 1745 era.

Iain Ghlinn Cuaich

"John of Glen Cuaich"
Gaelic Song Air on Bb

Fiddle setting by Aonghas Grant

This is a typical song of a girl lamenting for her lover. Though he's left her with child and gone away with somebody else, she still loves him, John of the long fair hair. Lynn Shevitz did the original transcription, at Stirling University.

It's a job playing these tunes because most of the Highland fiddlers typically never play the same speed, even twice. This is probably why the frustrated guy wrote "freely" on it. One minute we're away with it, then we slow it down, then there are a lot of grace notes that are thrown in.

[Aonghas likes playing slow tunes without concentrating on the beat and the barlines; here are two slightly different transcriptions of the tune, one intentionally without barlines.–Ed.]

Iain Ghlinn Cuaich

"John of Glen Cuaich"
Gaelic Song Air on Bb

Fiddle setting by Aonghas Grant

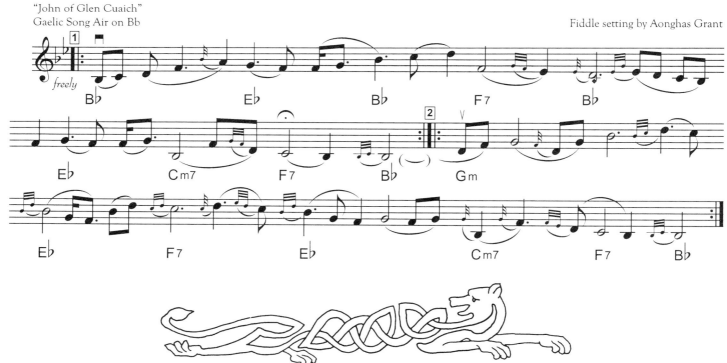

Chì Mi Muile

"I See Mull" ❖ The Land of my Youth
Gaelic Song Air on D

(♩ = 50)

By Donald MacLellan (20th cent.)
Setting by Aonghas Grant

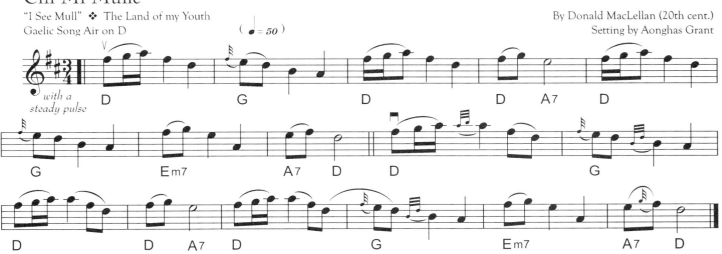

Chì Mi Muile

"I See Mull" ❖ The Land of my Youth
Gaelic Song Air on G

(♩ = 50)

By Donald MacLellan (20th cent.)
Setting by Aonghas Grant

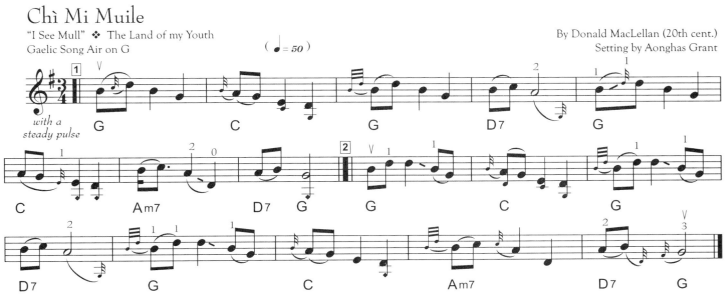

From Oban, looking at Kerrera, across the Firth of Lorne,
with Mull in the distance, 1984

An Chuilfhin
"The Coolin"
Irish Song Air on G

Setting by Aonghas Grant

An old Irish air. The Coolin was a way of braiding the Irishmen's hair, which was banned by the English in the 1600s.

This was originally written out from my playing by Lynn Shevitz at Stirling University in the 80s. I never could put in things like bars. Tom Anderson had a theory that in traditional music there was no such thing as bars—you could throw them out altogether.

[Above: the tune without details and without bars. Below: Laura Risk's detailed transcription of a recent performance by Aonghas.–Ed.]

An Chuilfhin
"The Coolin"
Irish Air on G

Setting by Aonghas Grant

It's a beautiful song, in Irish Gaelic—it's about a girl's lover. He was going to Dublin, and she pleaded with him to take his hair out of the pleat, before the soldiers got him. He said he'd wear the pleat in his own country. He was caught there and they hung him up in Dublin. This song is a lament for the lover who wore the pleat as an act of defiance.

I remember some years ago I was playing in Galway, and one of the great Irish singers, Mairi Ni Scolla, she was in her eighties then, she sang it. You could hear a pin drop. She was an old lady and she had the most beautiful quality to her voice, even at that age. For about five minutes after she sang, nobody could speak. It was really most moving.

Laoidh an t-Slanuighear

"Hymn to the Saviour"
Gaelic Song Air on G

(♩ = 44)

Setting by Aonghas Grant

This is in Captain Simon Fraser's *Knockie Collection of Highland Music* of 1816 which we worked a lot with, as he was a friend of my great-grandfather's. He was born at Ardachy, Stratherrick, and then moved to a place called Knockie about three miles away at the south side of the glen, above Loch Ness. He was an excellent player and a man of good education—he spoke French, Latin and English, a smattering of Greek as well as his native Gaelic. He was a great chess player—he liked nothing better than a game of chess and he was very difficult to beat. It was his father who mostly collected the songs, who used to go around buying cattle. The drovers used to go up to his father selling cattle, and they were all very interested in the songs and the music. Fraser says in his book that he hadn't collected the music himself, though it's quite well-known that he collected bits and pieces. He was a very talented musician and he obviously had been taught well by some person, because he's got cadenza runs and harmonics and double stops and things like that, all quite above the average. His music is predominantly of the period 1745, the Jacobite Rebellion rising.

My uncle used to play a version of this, though slightly different from what's written here. Fraser changed a lot of these tunes that were in the modal keys, introducing accidentals—sharps—that some of us don't play at all. A lot of people think that when he sent the manuscript down to Nathaniel Gow to be published, there were further revisions—the Gows altered some of the tunes to tidy them up.

[About the first grace note in the fourth bar of the second part: The first C is natural. Aonghas plays the remainder of the gracing with a straightened second finger and the next two Cs are closer to a C#.–Ed.]

The 16th-century Church at Trumpan, Waternish, Isle of Skye

O Luaidh

"Oh My Dearest Dear"
Gaelic Song Air on D

(♩. = 52)

Setting by Aonghas Grant

Guma Slàn a Chì Mi mo Chailin Dìleas Donn

"Health to my faithful brown-haired maid" ❖ Well may I behold my brown-haired maid
Gaelic Air on F

(♩. = 48)

Setting by Aonghas Grant

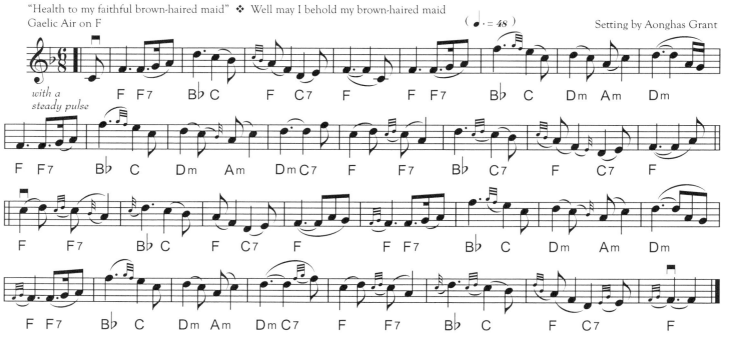

From the *Knockie Collection* and Patrick McDonald's *Collection*.

Tàladh Chriosda

"Christ Child Lullaby"
Gaelic Song Air on A

(♩. = 42)

Setting by Aonghas Grant

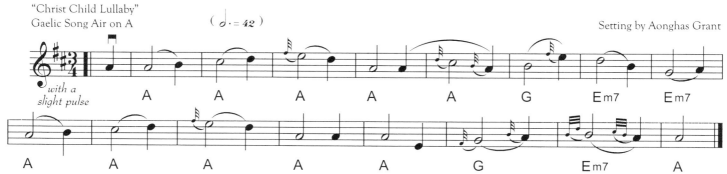

We used to play it at Christmas time. It's a nice wee tune, a good beginner's tune. The Gaelic words are by Fr. Allan MacDonald. He was a parish priest on Eriskay and a great collector of the island songs and stories. He was a native of Fort William, and was only in his forties when he died in 1905. The tune is an old one from Eriskay.

Crodh Laoigh nam Bodach

Carle's Cows ❖ "Old Men's Young Cattle"
Gaelic Song Air on E

(♩. = 30)

Setting by Aonghas Grant

Seconds—Crodh Laoigh nam Bodach

Seconds by Barbara McOwen

It's the ground of an old Pibroch. *[Both the* Knockie Collection *and the* Gesto Collection *subtitle this tune "The Plunder of the Lowlands now graze in the glens."–Ed.]*

Highland cattle

Bidh Clann Ulaidh

The Men of Ulster ❖ "The Clan MacAuley"
Gaelic Song Air on E

(♩. = 38)

Setting by Aonghas Grant

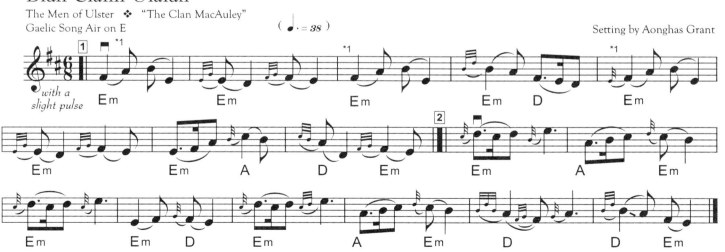

I would say it's taken from a pibroch tune, but it's more of a lullaby. It's about the MacAuleys. The nurse is singing to the child, "The men of Ulster will be dancing at your wedding." It's a nice wee tune–a great beginner's piece. It's sung on Skye. I heard it when I was very young.

*1

Moladh Beinn Dòbhrain

"In Praise of Ben Dorain"
Gaelic Song Air on G

Setting by Aonghas Grant

[Aonghas slips between a dotted 6/8 feel
and a cut-time feel in this part.—Ed.]

Ben Dorain on the left with "knuckles" *[Photo by David H. Arnold, 2002]*

Ben Dorain is a high mountain near Glenorchy. One version of the name is Hill of the Otter, while it is more likely Ben Dorn, the Hill of the Knuckle, having 4 small peaks like knuckles of a clenched fist. Duncan Bàn MacIntyre (1724–1812) was a famous bard, well-liked. In his youth he was a deer hunter and a lot of his songs were about mountain, stream and deer. This tune is formed on the basis of a pibroch. The tune was first transcribed from my playing by Fabrizzo Pilu, from Tuscany in Italy. He came twice to Stirling Summer School, a fine fiddler, loved Scottish fiddle music, always inviting me to Tuscany, never made it yet.

Maighdeannan na h-Àirigh

The Shieling Song ❖ "Maiden of the Shieling" ❖ Thug min' Oidhche Raoir san Àirigh

Gaelic Song Air on G

(♩ = 52)

Setting by Aonghas Grant

Seconds—Maighdeannan na h-Àirigh

Seconds by Allan Henderson

Double Stops—Maighdeannan na h-Àirigh

Fiddle setting by Aonghas Grant

It's said to have been made by a piper, a MacGillivray, in Glenaladale, Moidart, who left for Cape Breton.

The sheiling was the place in the summer time, the very happy period when predominantly all the young people went away up to the high glens and corries and herded the cattle and sheep right through to the autumn. They stayed in little bothies. You still see the ruins everywhere in the glens. It was a great time for music and piping and dancing and a lot of good tunes and songs came out of that period. In the autumn, they took their cattle and sheep back down to the low ground.

We usually play it with stops and harmonize it that way. And some ones of us play it high. It could also be played as a waltz, but it would be different:

Etc.

An Ataireachd Àrd

The High Surge of the Sea ❖ The Eternal Surge of the Sea

Gaelic Song Air on G

By John MacDonald (20th cent.)

Fiddle setting by Aonghas Grant

$(\, . = 24 \,)$

Seconds—An Ataireachd Àrd

Seconds by Allan Henderson

This tune is by John MacDonald of Oban, and the words are by Donald MacIvor, a schoolteacher on the Isle of Lewis. A person is returning to his boyhood village, now deserted and in ruins. The sea breaking and surging on the rocks is the only thing that remains the same as his childhood. The Seconds is by one of my best pupils, Allan Henderson, now with Blazin' Fiddles. We can follow this with a jig [e.g. "Black-Haired Girl of Knockie," p.100]—you get a good clout when you come off a slow air with a jig. That's what we always used to do at home.

The Butt of Lewis

Moladh na Lanndaidh

"In Praise of Islay"
Gaelic Song Air on D   (𝅗𝅥 = 46)   Setting by Aonghas Grant

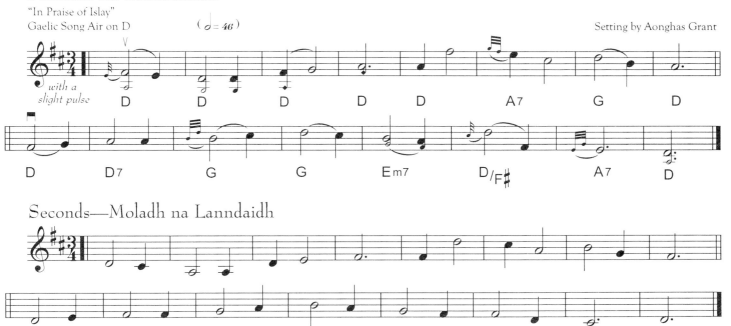

Seconds—Moladh na Lanndaidh

It's in D for the students. When I'm playing it myself I usually play it in Eb.

Òganaich an Òr-fhuilt Bhuidhe

"The Young One with the Golden Locks"
Gaelic Song Air on D   (𝅗𝅥 = 38)   Setting by Aonghas Grant

A couple of years ago Ruairidh Peter Campbell of Barra was doing a CD of this song with Paddy Shaw on the box, myself on fiddle, and Ruairidh on flute. The song is about a girl who is in love with a hunter. She can hear his gunshots in the hills, then learns he is leaving the place and she is heartbroken. If he leaves her, her hair will turn gray.

Gruagach Òg an Fhuilt Bhàin

"The Fair Maid of Barra"
Gaelic Song Air on D

(♩. = 30)

By Donald J. Campbell (20th cent.)
Setting by Aonghas Grant

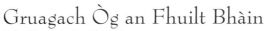

This was for Morag MacAuley of Castlebay. She just died two or three years ago. Apparently she was a very beautiful girl. Eventually she had a lot of suitors, but she never got married. It was Donald Allan MacDonald, the bard from South Uist, that composed the words.

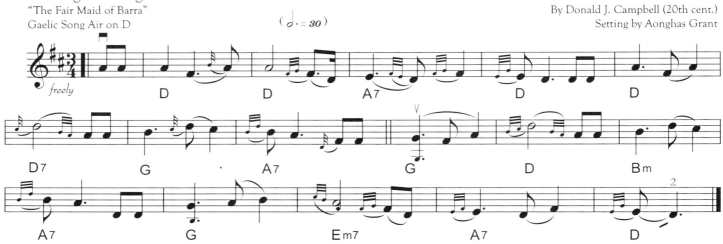

Kisimul Castle, Castlebay, Barra *[Photo by Michael Rowen, 2005]*

Soraidh Slàn le Fionnairidh

"Farewell to Fiunary"
Gaelic Song Air on G

(♩. = 50)

Setting by Aonghas Grant

Seconds—Soraidh Slàn le Fionnairidh

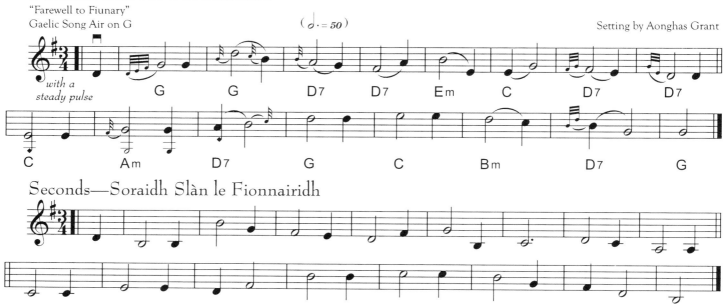

[The words to this song were written by Rev. Dr. Norman MacLeod (1783–1862), known as the "Friend of the Gaels" and the "Father of Gaelic Prose." He grew up in Fiunary, on the Morvern coast opposite Mull, but had to leave for school and work. The pier at Fiunary was also the emigration point for the many Highlanders in the area who left during the Clearances.—Ed.]

An Còineachan

Hò-Bhan Hò-Bhan ❖ Fairy Lullaby
Gaelic Song Air on G

(♩. = 40)

Setting by Aonghas Grant

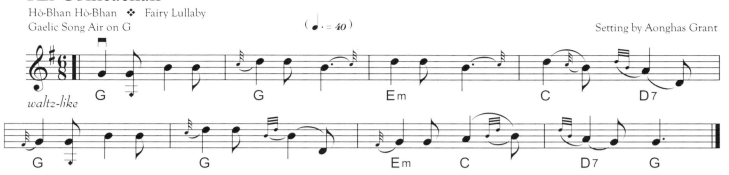

waltz-like

An Còineachan

Hò-Bhan Hò-Bhan ❖ Fairy Lullaby
Gaelic Song Air on A

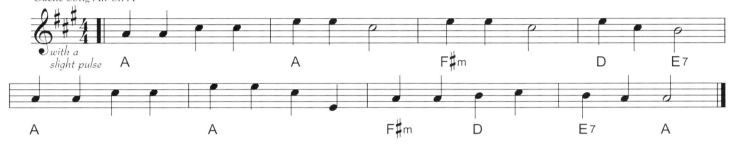

with a slight pulse

This is *the* beginners' tune, the Gaelic equivalent of "Twinkle Twinkle Little Star." The words—she has her baby with her, then she puts the baby down and goes to gather blaeberries. When she came back, she'd found the fairies had stolen her baby. She'd discovered the little brown otter's tracks, but never discovered her baby-o.

[Here are two settings of the same tune—different keys, different meters.—Ed.]

Tha mi Tìnn Leis a' Ghaol

"My Mind is of Love" ❖ "The Languor of Love"
Gaelic Song Air on D

(♩ = 50)

Setting by Aonghas Grant

freely

Mo Rùn Geal Òg

A Lady to her Husband who was killed at the Battle of Culloden ❖ "My dearest fair-haired young one"
Gaelic Song Air on E

Setting by Aonghas Grant

Mo Rùn Geal Òg

A Lady to her Husband who was killed at the Battle of Culloden ❖ "My dearest fair-haired young one"
Gaelic Song Air on E

Setting by Aonghas Grant

This is a famous Gaelic song. "Mo Rùn Geal Òg" is an endearment term, meaning "my dearest fair-haired young one." It's a peculiar tune, the way it's played, it seems to be done in wee bursts. At the top is Fraser's version from the *Knockie Collection*. The bottom version is based on singing with Gaelic words.

The "Lady" is Christine Fergusson, whose husband never came back from Culloden. She was working in Erchless Castle. When she was old she stayed with a farmer up in Glenurquhart. When she died, at this time Erchless Castle was a ruin, and the farmer got a nice big lintel stone from the castle and put it as her gravestone, and it's written on it "Fergusson, Mo rùn geal òg, 1746." It's in the glen but I'm not sure where. She's blaming Charlie for the death of her husband—it starts out "Young Charlie Stewart, you've taken everything away that I love."

Those were some sad times, a lot of dashed hopes. I've often wondered, if Charlie had never come across the sea, how things would have happened. I think a lot of people would have left anyway, the glens were getting too crowded, the old clan system was starting to fade out. The changes would have come, except they wouldn't have been half so brutal as after the aftermath of Culloden. The only thing which saved a lot of them from dying was it happened in the springtime—their houses were burnt down and their cattle taken away, so they had the summer to get themselves together again.

Marches

Bonnie Ann
2/4 Pipe March on A

By Duncan Ross (19th cent.)
Fiddle setting by Aonghas Grant

We would play 2/4 marches for dances—for barn dances. We would speed them up a wee bit. In some cases the pipers would play 2/4 marches slightly slower than fiddlers.

[In choosing a March-Strathspey-Reel set for competition or performance, Aonghas often uses a 2/4 pipe march as the march.— Ed.]

The Highland Wedding

2/4 Pipe March on A

(♩ = 76)

Pipe setting by P/M Angus MacKay (1813-59)
Fiddle setting by Aonghas Grant

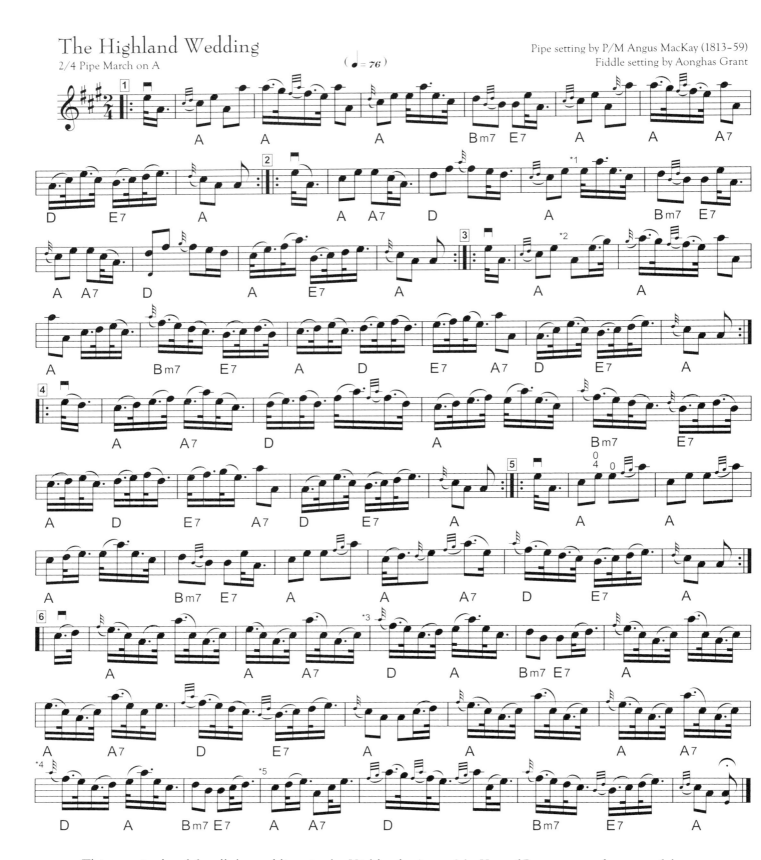

This tune is played for all the weddings in the Highlands. Angus MacKay, of Raasay, was taken out of the army to be First Piper to Queen Victoria. He was attributed to be one of the first to write down the pipe music into musical notation from the Gaelic vocables—canntaireachd.

36

Corrieyairack

2/4 Pipe March on A

(♩ = 69)

By Aonghas Grant
Setting by Aonghas Grant

Whitebridge, south side of Loch Ness. The sign on the right reads: "The White Bridge—One of the best examples of a hump-backed single span Wade bridge crossing the River Fechlin, and carrying the military road engineered in 1732 - date on bridge - by Major Caulfield, Roads Inspector under General Wade. This famous route linked the Hanoverian barrack-forts of Inverness and Kilcumein, now Fort Augustus. Hotel is on or near site of a King's House.—Inverness Field Club, 1973"

This is one of the first tunes I wrote, in about 1956. It was transcribed in 1976 by Willie Lawrie of Kinlochleven, who played the piano and box on the Topic LP—*Highland Fiddle*—and is the grandson of Pipe Major Willie Lawrie. Corrieyairack is a high pass, and General Wade's military road goes up through it, and it takes you over into Ruthven Barracks in Strathspey from Ft. Augustus. It's in the Culachy Estate, where I worked as a shepherd in my young days. We used to take motorbikes over it. We'd put on our Welly boots, carry our shoes in a bag, and go to dances in Newtonmore. When they put the electricity in, with all the big American Army Studebaker lorries coming in, they built the pylons up following the road because it was so well-engineered. Although Wade got the credit, it was a Major Caulfield who did most of the work. Some of his bridges, particularly the Corrieyairack one, it's amazing—it's a 200-year-old stone arched bridge, and it withstood all the lorries going over it all those years.

Dungarthill

2/4 Pipe March on A

By James Macintosh (1846–1937)

The Dunkeld Bridge over the River Tay at Dunkeld.
The Dungarthill Estate is just outside Dunkeld.

Colonel McLean of Ardgour

2/4 Pipe March on D ♩. = 69

By P/M John McLellan, DCM (Dunoon) (1875–1949)

Fiddle setting by Aonghas Grant

The MacLeans have been Chiefs in Sunart/Ardgour for a very long time. The last one, Miss MacLean, died a few years ago. The Estate has now been divided up, with some parts sold. Some relations still have parts of it. "Ardgour" means "the high point of the goats"—at one time there were large herds of wild goats.

At Assembly Rooms, Edinburgh Fiddle Festival 2004: Tribute Concert for Farquhar MacRae with Ross Martin, Iain MacFarlane, Aonghas, Charlie MacFarlane, Allan MacDonald, Fergie MacDonald

[Photo by Stan Reeves]

The Braes of Castle Grant

2/4 Pipe March on A

Parts 1 & 2 by Duncan MacDonald (pub. 1863)
Parts 3 & 4 by George S. McLennan (1884–1929)
Fiddle setting by Aonghas Grant

(♩ = 72)

Duncan MacDonald was the piper to the Laird of Grant, in Grantown. These were the Strathspey Grants, the main clan. Away back in the 1100s one of the Chiefs of the Grants married one of the daughters of the MacDonnells in Glenmoriston, and then eventually the Grants became the prominent clan in the glen (Glenmoriston), but they were just a branch of the main clan. We were the Grants that got mixed up with the Jacobite rising, everything got burnt down, and it was my great-great-great grandfather and his brother that got deported to Barbados and never seen again.

This was composed in the 1800s. Then G.S. MacLennan added the 3rd & 4th parts—he did such a good job at it, you'd think it was just done by the one person. Donald MacLeod was another great man at adding the two extra parts.

Paardeberg

2/4 Pipe March on D (♩ = 72)   Fiddle setting by Aonghas Grant

Hector MacDonald, the Highland General, was born near Dingwall. He was the only Gaelic speaking General, and the Establishment hated him, because he was just one of the local crofter boys, but a great soldier, and he was the only private in the history of the British Army that rose from the ranks of a private to a general. [He fought in several wars leading up to the Boer War, and commanded the Highland Brigade at the Battle of Paardeberg, in February 1900.–Ed.]

After the Boer War he was a great favourite of the Prince of Wales, and he was dispatched to Ceylon. His wife couldn't stand the heat, and she came home to Edinburgh. He was a pretty lonely guy; he used to go out fishing and shooting, and would take one of the Indian servant boys along with him. The other officers began putting it round that he was gay, that he was having a liaison with this young Indian. Of course in those days that was fatal. Eventually he was supposed to have blown his brains out in a hotel room in Paris. He's buried in St. Giles, Edinburgh. Trevor Royle just recently wrote a book about him. "Fighting Mac," the boys used to call him. He was great with the Highland regiments because he'd ride along on his horse and shout them up in Gaelic. They fought harder because he was one of them. Sad end, whatever's the truth in that. There's a memorial for him outside Dingwall. And "Hector the Hero" is one of Skinner's great tunes.

Mrs Cameron-Head of Inverailort

2/4 Pipe March on A

By Johnnie MacKinnon (d. ca. 1985)

Mrs Pauline Cameron-Head of Inverailort Castle was my employer for many years, when I was a shepherd and deerstalker. As a boy I was at her wedding in 1942. Over fifty years later I was also at her funeral in Arisaig. She was renowned for her kindness to the local people. Johnnie MacKinnon was a carpenter and a fine piper. When he was old he made a bag for his pipes which was blown up by an old vacuum motor plugged into a light socket.

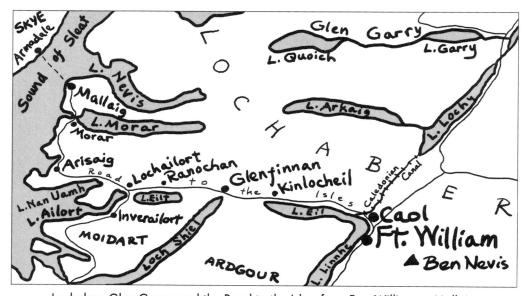

Lochaber, Glen Garry, and the Road to the Isles, from Fort William to Mallaig

Father Michael's Farewell to Lochyside School

2/4 Pipe March on A

By Aonghas Grant
Setting by Aonghas Grant

Father Michael MacDonald was the Parish Priest at home, and used to be at the school where my wife worked. He was shifting to South Uist, and Violet Smith, the teacher at the school, thought it would be lovely if I could compose a tune for him, because he's a good singer himself and he liked music. A few years back he was 25 years a Priest, so they had a Silver Jubilee for him, and they asked me to play this tune. They had a big open-air ceremony—it was a beautiful day and they had 600-700 people at it, of various denominations, and 6 priests at this altar outside. There was a choir on the side, with mikes up, and a mike for me. It was arranged, right after the choir finished singing, that I start playing this tune. The procession started down towards the altar, with the incense, and just as they stopped, and he bowed to the altar, I finished the tune! It couldn't have been planned better. One of the other priests there was a piper as well, and after the ceremony and all the food and drink, he had some of the pipers playing this—it's lovely to hear this played on the pipes.

Davie Arbuthnott

2/4 Pipe March on A

($\quad = 72$)

By Aonghas Grant
Setting by Aonghas Grant

Davie came to Stirling Summer Schools every year. He became a very good friend and was always a great help in anything that was needed done in class. He was in every class, Tom Anderson's and Alastair Hardie's. Tom wrote an Air for him, called "The Cornerstone," which he was indeed. Sadly, Davie took a stroke and can no longer play. He was a staunch member for many years with the Stirling Caledonian Strathspey & Reel Society. I composed this while at Stirling in 1984, and it was written out that same year by Chris Maskell.

Aonghas with Highland fiddle class, Stirling University, July 1982. Davie is on the far left, and the wee boy in the middle up top is the now-famous fiddler Gavin Marwick

Teuch Chaw

"Tough Chew"
2/4 March on D

By Robert Stewart (d. 1959)

Composed by Robert (Secky) Stewart's grandfather Robert—himself a piper during World War I. The Teuch Chaw, which is Scots for Tough Chew, related to the army biscuits known as Iron Rations (or hard tack) as they would break your teeth, they were so hard. The only way to eat them was to soak them in water or tea, both rather scarce in the trenches in France.

Tammy's March

4/4 March on F

(♩ = *104*)

By Aonghas Grant

[Aonghas' return tribute to Tom Anderson. See the fine 6/8 march which Tom wrote for Aonghas on page 53.–Ed.]

Cabar Fèidh

"Deer's Antlers"
4/4 Pipe March on G or A

(♩ = 108)

Setting by Aonghas Grant

*3 - Transition to Strathspey

"Cabar Fèidh," or the "deer's antlers," are on the coat of arms of the MacKenzies of Kintail. This came about when Alexander III was hunting in the Mar Forest. This was in 1265. A stag was chased by the hounds and charged the king, when MacKenzie shot the stag in the head with an arrow. He was granted the stag's antlers as the armorial bearing for saving the king's life. The Mar Forest is over Deeside, and the king would often have people with him from the various clans. The Cabar Fèidh is also used by the Seaforth Highlanders, the Highland regiment of the British Army.

[The tune "Cabar Fèidh" appears in this collection four times—as a 4/4 March, a Strathspey, a Reel and a Jig (see pages 70, 71 and 97). Many Scottish tunes find themselves "transformed" from one meter and tempo to another, and this is one of the best-known of these versatile Highland tunes. Though "Cabar Fèidh" appears in many fiddle books as a two-part reel on C/D, Aonghas' versions are closer to the settings found in pipe books. He usually puts the four "Cabar Fèidhs" together as a set, moving from one to the next without a break.—Ed.]

David Arnold's Welcome to Scotland

4/4 March on D

(♩ = 96)

By Aonghas Grant

David H. Arnold interviewing Aonghas, Lochyside, February 2003

[David H. Arnold met Aonghas at the New Hampshire Highland Games in September 1998. They found they had several interests in common, one of them being that they each hope to complete the construction of his first violin. David helped launch this book project, and accompanied Barbara McOwen to Aonghas' home in Lochyside in February 2002 to collect the first batch of material. This was David's first trip to Scotland, and Aonghas wrote this tune during the visit to commemorate the fact. All of us are very grateful for the work and thought David contributed early on, and his ongoing interest and assistance.–Ed.]

Alex Stormonth

4/4 March on D

(♩ = *112*)

By Aonghas Grant
Setting by Aonghas Grant

A pupil and friend, Alex came for many years to my class at Stirling University. A fine fiddler, and a retired Police Inspector. Composed at Stirling University, July 1990.

The Battle of Waterloo

4/4 Pipe March on A

(♩ = *104*)

Setting by Aonghas Grant

It's unusual there, C natural. That's the way we always played it. I don't know whether it's right or not. This old boy, Alan Ross, I think, from Invergarry, used to play it like this, and everybody just followed his lead. We used to play this at dances, for the Gay Gordons. We'd speed it up a bit.

The Battle of Waterloo, July 1815, was Napoleon's last battle. Captain Cameron and a lot of the local boys were killed there. There's a big circle of pine trees planted for them, just down the road from here, in Fassiefearn.

A Favorite Quick Step

The Reverend John MacFarlane
Quickstep on D

(♩=76)

By Hugh Montgomery (1740–1819)
Setting by Aonghas Grant

[This tune was originally published by Nathaniel Gow in the book New Strathspey Reels ... Composed by a Gentleman, *known to be Hugh Montgomery, Earl of Eglinton, an amateur violinist and friend of the Gows.–Ed.]*

Aonghas with the Intermediate Class at the first Boston Harbor Scottish Fiddle School, Thompson Island, Boston, Mass., August 2003

King Jamie's March

Quickstep on G

(♩=88)

Setting by Aonghas Grant

From *The Inverness Collection*. A very old tune for one of the Scottish King James. The last one, James VII, was Prince Charlie's father.

The Knocking Wheel
Quickstep on G

By Sue Jones

Seconds—The Knocking Wheel

Seconds by Catriona Thompson

Sue and Catriona are two friends of mine who have been at Stirling many times. Sue has composed quite a number of tunes. This was after a spinning wheel course where the wheel seemed to knock every turn. Sue lives in Chester, Catriona is from Edinburgh. Composed at Stirling, 1998.

The Boyne Water
Quickstep on A   (♩ = 72)

Setting by Aonghas Grant

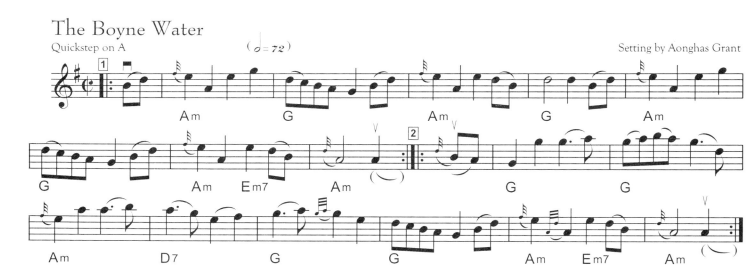

I got this from *The Inverness Collection*, and it says, "Lochaber version." The Battle of the Boyne took place in Ireland in 1690. It caused all the havoc over there, and all the Orange boys still celebrate in July, with the bands marching through Belfast.

The Hills of Glengarry

6/8 March on A

(♩. = 92)

By Aonghas Grant
Setting by Aonghas Grant

Loch Garry in Winter

I was coming back from playing at a dance in Kintail; this was 30 years ago. I was getting pretty tired so I thought I'd stop at the top of the pass in Glengarry. It was a beautiful morning and I got out and had a little walk around to sort of freshen myself up and actually splashed my face in a stream and I was looking at all the hills way up to Glen Quoich. You could see way over to my great-grandfather's house across the loch, Loch Garry, and all the hills around. I thought "The Hills of Glengarry"—good name for a tune, and by the time I'd gone five minutes down the road I had the whole thing in my head. I got home and I played it and that was it.

Originally transcribed by John White, the brass teacher at Lochaber High School.

The Heights of Cassino

By P/M Dan MacRae (d. 1985)
Setting by Aonghas Grant

6/8 Pipe March on D

In the 3rd part, the pipes hang onto the long A, while fiddlers tend to fill in with 3 A's. They often do that—it keeps the rhythm better. Monte Cassino is a place above Naples. A lot of the Scots boys from around here were killed there trying to capture it during the war. Eventually the Poles came in and managed to get it. There was a beautiful monastery there but it was smashed to bits in the battles.

*1 - Transition between parts

Aonghas at a session at Valley of the Moon Scottish Fiddling School, California, ca. 1992
[Photo by Cherry Clark]

Angus Grant's Welcome to Shetland

6/8 March on A

By Tom Anderson (1910–1991)

[Reproduced by permission of Shetland Musical Trust]

Tom Anderson was the most prolific composer of the 20th century in Scotland. Many of his tunes come up to the highest level of any composer. He's most famous for "Da Slockit Light," and he wrote many very good reels, marches, jigs and slow airs.

Tom Anderson, Stirling University, July 1982
[Photo: courtesy Arlene Leitch Patterson archives]

Pipe Major Sam Scott

6/8 Pipe March on D

By P/M Peter R. MacLeod (1878–1965)
Fiddle setting by Aonghas Grant

(♩. = 100)

Portree Bay, Isle of Skye

Portree Bay

By John L. MacKenzie (19th cent.)
Setting by Aonghas Grant

6/8 March on A

[*Aonghas opens the 1977 Topic LP* Highland Fiddle *with the set "Pipe Major Sam Scott" and "Portree Bay." It would also work well to add "Angus MacKinnon" in the middle for a three-tune set.—Ed.*]

Angus MacKinnon

By P/M Donald Shaw Ramsay (1919–1998)
Setting by Aonghas Grant

6/8 Pipe March on B

Murdo MacKenzie of Torridon

6/8 Pipe March on A

By Bobby MacLeod (1925–1991)

Aonghas with Bobby MacLeod at the Dunvegan Festival, 1978;
in back are Farquhar MacRae (partially hidden), Bruce Turnbull,
A. MacDonald [Photo by Carrole Bennett]

The Maids of Kintail

The Grey Buck ❖ The Loving Black Lad
6/8 Pipe March on A

(♩. = 88)

Setting by Aonghas Grant

"The Maids of Kintail" are the Five Sisters, mountain peaks along Glen Shiel in Kintail. This tune seems to have gone out of fashion a bit. I've heard pipers play it as a jig.

Lochanside

Retreat March on D

By P/M John McLellan, DCM (Dunoon) (1875–1949)
Setting by Aonghas Grant

Seconds—Lochanside

Seconds by Hazel Copeland

Retreat Marches, or Retreat Airs, are typically in 3/4 or 9/8. They're played at the end of the day, when the soldiers retire to their barracks. They're the closest thing to a waltz that they have in the Highlands.

'Pibroch' MacKenzie's Farewell

Retreat March on D

By James Ross Riddell (1913–2005)

Setting by Aonghas Grant

(♩. = 96)

Aonghas' Riddell fiddle

Alex (Pibroch) MacKenzie was the fiddler for many years with Bobby MacLeod's band. I think I got this tune from the Inverness boys. Jimmy Riddell played the double bass in the Highland Strathspey and Reel Society. He was also a piper, and he was brother to the more famous Donald Riddell, who made lots of fiddles—I've got one of them. All the famous young fiddlers in that area were Donald's pupils—Bruce MacGregor, Duncan Chisholm, Gregor Borland, to name just three. Jimmy passed on just recently.

This fiddle *[shown at left]* was made for me in the 60s by my friend Donald Riddell, the famous fiddler, composer and fiddle maker. It's a very fine fiddle. The back of it is sycamore from a tree that was lying down at Lord Lovat's Castle at Beaufort, near Beauly. The front is a bit of bog pine that came out of a peat bog, pulled up by the Forestry ploughs. He saved some of it, and cut it to make fiddle fronts. It's very, very close-grained. He sent a bit of it to get carbon-tested in Aberdeen, and they weren't too sure, but they thought it was at least 10,000 years old. It had been preserved in the peat since the last ice age.

Dream Valley of Glendaruel

Retreat March on D

(♩ = 100)

Setting by Aonghas Grant

Seconds—Dream Valley of Glendaruel

Seconds by Hazel Copeland

*1 - INTRO

A good way to get into the tune is to play a couple of bars as an Intro. The 3/4 marches make lovely duets for two people to play together. We often jump down and play the tune on the back strings.

Kilworth Hills

Retreat March on A

(♩ = 104)

By P/M George S. McLennan (1883-1929)
Setting by Aonghas Grant

*1

Far Over Struy

Retreat March on D

By John Peter MacLeod (1871-1920)
Setting by Aonghas Grant

Heights of Dargai

Retreat March on A

By J. Wallace (d. 1912)
Setting by Aonghas Grant

Seconds—Heights of Dargai

Seconds by Mike Hardcastle

Dargai was an epic battle involving the Highland regiments in India in the 1800s. Scott Skinner also wrote a Pibroch of the same name. Mike Hardcastle is a good friend from Sussex; he came for some years to the Stirling Summer School. He is a fine fiddler who knows a lot of old English folk tunes. Mike also plays the pipes. I think he is really a Scot at heart.

When the Battle is Over

Retreat March on A

(♩ = 104)

By P/M William Robb (d. 1942)
Setting by Aonghas Grant

*1 - grace notes for the very last time:

Herbie MacLeod and Aonghas at Herbie's "welcoming"
home, Arlington, Massachusetts, 1998

Memories of Herbie MacLeod

Retreat March on G

By Aonghas Grant

Setting by Aonghas Grant

Seconds—Memories of Herbie MacLeod

Seconds by Barbara McOwen

[Herbie MacLeod of Arlington, Massachusetts, was a close friend of Aonghas', though they met only a handful of times in person. Herbie and Marjorie's home was a Cape Breton Central; though crowded enough with seven children, it was always open to any fiddler passing through town. The late Dan R. MacDonald came for an overnight stop and stayed for weeks. Aonghas had several nice visits with Herbie during a trip to the States in September 1998. They listened to Herbie's house party tapes, went out for meals with friends, and Herbie's son Jim took them up on a drive to the North Shore. Another son, known as Little Herbie, set up his own room in the house for an overnight stay by Aonghas. Aonghas played fiddle with Charlie, another of Herbie's sons, at the piano at the Canadian American Club in Watertown. Herbie died in May 2000.—Ed.]

He's Mr. Highland. His parents were Gaelic-speaking people from Cape Breton and his father's people came from the Highlands way back in the 1800s. Herbie lived *[in the Boston area]* for years, and worked for the Transport for the city. He had a big family; one of his daughters, Helen, is a Senator in California, married to Cap Thomson, Pate's brother. One son is Jim MacLeod, and he's a manager in the Canadian Club. Another daughter, from Rhode Island, is a colonel in the U.S. Army. I met Herbie at a Mod in Inverness 30 years ago. My wife came down with me, and we were there just for the day. I was playing a concert, and it's one of the few times she came down. She was a MacLeod, and wearing her tartan kilt, and we met this big guy in the doorway at the Cummings Hotel. He said, "Gee, you must be a MacLeod! I'm Herbie MacLeod from Boston, I'm always delighted to meet a MacLeod!" And he talked away. Then this other guy, Donnie MacBeth, a fiddler from Aberdeen who knew Herbie, said, "Have you met Aonghas Grant, the fiddler?" "Gee, are you a fiddler?" And he talked away, now that he knew I played the fiddle. We met for just a few hours there, and that was it. Then there were letters and tapes, the *Cape Breton Highlander* newspaper, and phone calls. It's "Hold Fast" *[the Clan MacLeod motto]* and "Stand Fast" *[the Clan Grant motto]*.

The Highland Brigade at Magersfontein

By P/M John McLellan, DCM (Dunoon) (1875-1949)

Retreat March on A

Setting by Aonghas Grant

Seconds—The Highland Brigade at Magersfontein

Seconds by Hazel Copeland

One of the battles of the Boer War took place in the Magersfontein Hills. The casualties have always been kept quiet. When I was a boy, some of the old-timers had been out there—the officers of the British Army were still running about on white horses and in red coats, and the farmers there were great shots with the rifles, and they shot all the officers out of the saddles just like shooting bottles off a dyke. Later, the British Army burnt the farms and took all the women and children into concentration camps and the South Africans have never forgiven them for that.

Hazel Copeland, who wrote the Seconds, is a fine fiddler and accordion player who came to Stirling Summer School for a number of years. She was a great help to me with her knowledge of harmony.

Strathspeys and Reels

Because he was a bonnie Lad
Strathspey on A

(♩ = 69)

Setting by Aonghas Grant

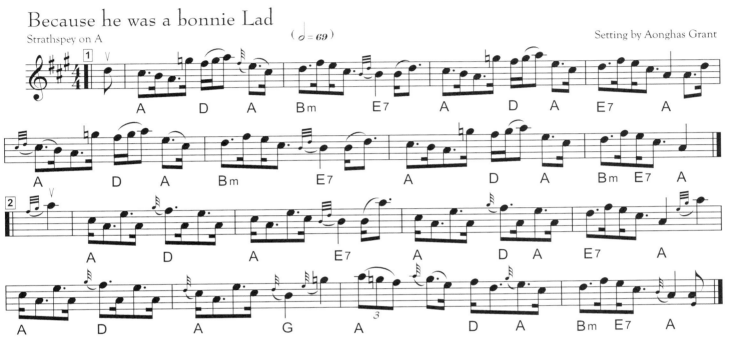

A traditional strathspey. The "bonnie lad" is Prince Charlie.

The Hurdle Race
Reel on A

(♩ = 96)

By James Fraser (1832–1895)
Setting by Aonghas Grant

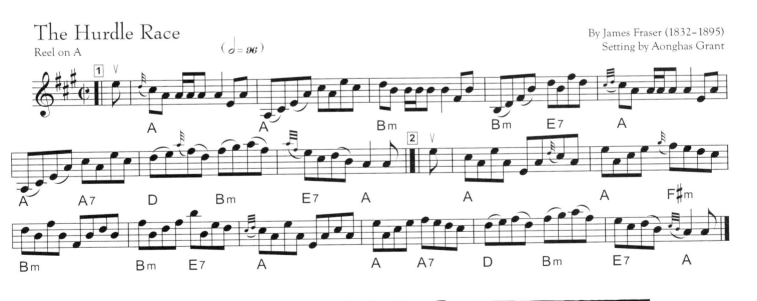

Morag's Wedding
Strathspey / Port-a-beul on A

$(\quarternote = 72)$

Setting by Aonghas Grant

Sometimes known as "Morag's Made a Wedding o't." This is a traditional port-a-beul (mouth music) strathspey.

*1 - Transition to Beginning

Scotsville Reel
Known in Scotland as "MacKinnon's Reel"
Reel on A

$(\quarternote = 108)$

By Allan MacFarlane (1878-1938)
Setting by Aonghas Grant

*1 - Alternate bowing on 3rd & 4th parts

etc.

I played this tune for years and years, always knew it as "MacKinnon's Reel." While preparing this book, we looked about for any sources of this tune, and we couldn't find it in any book. Finally Doug MacPhee gave us a copy out of Gordon MacQuarrie's *Cape Breton Collection of Scottish Melodies*. Allan MacFarlane, Rory MacKinnon and others were community pipers and played an older style of piping on Cape Breton Island, Nova Scotia.

If you go to the hill, take your gun

The Leys of Luncarty

Strathspey on A

($\quad$ = 66)

Setting by Aonghas Grant

This reel is another old one, from the 1715 Jacobite rising, when all the chiefs skinned out over the highway to Paris and left the poor Highlandmen to bear the brunt of it. It's the oldest known setting of it, probably the original setting, and no one's very sure who composed it. Even the setting in Gow's book is not this setting.

Comely Garden

Reel on A

($\quad$ = 88)

By Daniel Dow (1732-1783)

Setting by Aonghas Grant

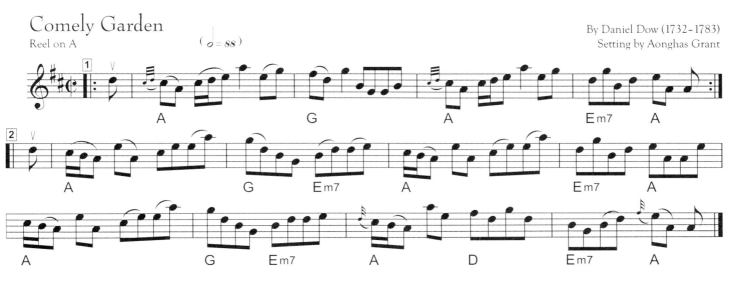

Tha Bean Agam, tha Taigh Agam

"I have a Wife, I have a House"
Strathspey / Port-a-beul on A

(♩ = **69**)

Setting by Aonghas Grant

This is a traditional strathspey, a port-a-beul, with somewhat comical Gaelic words. *[See the alternate setting in the key of D, page 82.]*

Bodaich Bheag Obar Itheachan

"The Little Men from Abriachan"
Strathspey / Port-a-beul on A

(♩ = **69**)

Setting by Aonghas Grant

Abriachan *(pron. a-BREE-a-khan)* is a little town in the mountains above Loch Ness, in the Great Glen. There's a very old story behind this tune. There were three small men—I'm not sure if they were brothers or related—they went away to a funeral. They were away for days, and making their way home with the drink, they fell in bogs and burns. Somebody composed a very comic song about their activities. Unfortunately, most of the song is lost, it was so long ago, and it's been turned into a strathspey over the years. *[Other names for this tune are "Ca' the Stirks frae out the corn" (Skye Collection) and "The Highlanders Farewell to Ireland" (Gow's 2nd Repository), and it is very similar to the reel "Coming thro the Broom my Jo" (below).—Ed.]*

*1 - Alternate Bowings:

Coming thro the Broom my Jo

Reel on A

"Jo" is an old Scots term of endearment to a loved one. "Broom" is a very soft flowering bush. The tune refers to a lovers' meeting, and was published in Bremner's *Collection* in 1757.

Null Thar nan Eileanan

"Over the Isles to America"
Reel / Port-a-beul on A

This is a traditional reel. There are also Gaelic song words to this tune, sung as a port-a-beul.

The strathspeys in puirt-a-beul are very quick. Some people have the idea that that's where the strathspeys originated, from the Gaelic puirt-a-beul. It's hard to say though—there are other stories. It's said there was a drunken fiddler at a wedding in Strathspey. He got filled up with so much drink he couldn't play the reels fast, so he played them slow and someone said, "That sounds good!" That's only a story, I think. One of the first ones to play strathspeys was Angus Cumming, from Grantown. It was Bremner's *Collection* in 1757 which had "strathspey reels." I think it just evolved. It's certainly one of two forms of native music—the strathspey on the fiddle and the pibroch on the pipes. Jigs and reels and airs and so on are all over everywhere, but when you think of Scotland, you think of strathspeys.

The port-a-beul is mouth music, it's for the days when you haven't got any instrumental music at all, and people just sang that for dancing. I remember this old friend of mine, he was a station master for years, John Monaghan, he was of Irish extraction—one time when he was a young fellow he went over to see his relations in Ireland. They were saying, "Are you staying for the dance?! On Friday night, it'll be a great night, Seamus will be there himself, the great Seamus." So he was looking forward to it. He arrived up at the school, and there was this old guy sitting in a chair in the corner, with a glass of whisky, and everyone was going up to him and being very deferential. Suddenly he was up, doing "Diddlie dae do diddly ro ho dum." And that was the band! He diddled all night—jigs, reels. He was famous for diddling and he could go for hours.

There are some competitions sponsored by the TMSA (Traditional Music & Song Association) for Scottish music and song, and Davie Glen—a big long beard, a great character—he put a cup in, then won it himself, he was so good. He used to have the dancing dolly—on the knee—he'd be diddling and dancing the dolly at the same time. It was a great act.

Cabar Fèidh

"The Deer's Antlers"
Strathspey on A

$(\quad = 72)$

Setting by Aonghas Grant

Although people call it staghorn, it's really bone. Sheep's horn is a horn, which is a totally different thing. The sheep don't cast the horn, whereas the stags cast the antlers every year. I would imagine it takes a lot out of the stag to grow a set of horns. The young ones haven't so many points. As they get older they're big and they have what they call brows and bays. Some are beautiful symmetrical heads, and others are not so good. Away over in Blair Castle, when people see all the antlers in the hall, they think of all the poor beasts that they think got slaughtered. The cast antlers are very useful—you can use them for handles for sticks and knives.

"Cabar Fèidh" is a very versatile tune—it can be played as a march, a strathspey, a reel and a jig. It is originally a Gaelic song and it is the Rallying Song of the MacKenzies of Kintail.

Cabar Fèidh

"The Deer's Antlers"
Reel on A

($\quad$ = 120)

Setting by Aonghas Grant

"Red deer stags in winter with the snow level well down on the hills."
—Lea MacNally, *Highland Year*, Pan Books, 1968

Duchess of Athole

Strathspey on A

By Niel Gow (1727–1807)

Captain Ross's Reel

Reel on A

(♩ = 88)

Setting by Aonghas Grant

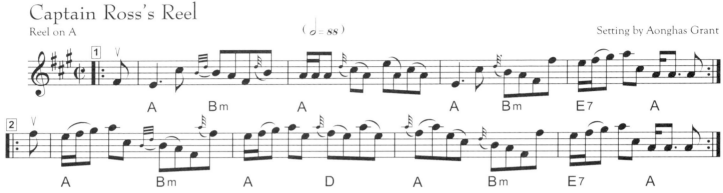

This is an old traditional tune from Bremner's *Collection* of 1730.

Captain MacDuff

Reel on A

By Daniel Dow (1732–1783)

Setting by Aonghas Grant

Aonghas working for the Ranger Service, unloading culvert pipes
for the Ben Nevis trail, ca. 1993 *[Photo by Hugh MacNally]*

J.F. Mackenzie Esqr. of Garrynahine, Stornoway

Strathspey on A

By W.J. Ross, Soval (20th cent.)
Setting by Aonghas Grant

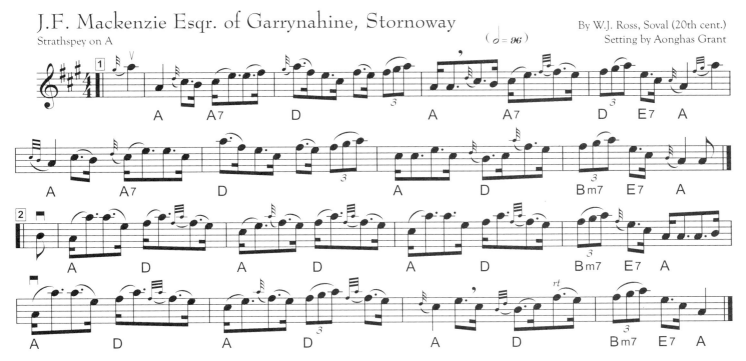

[Aonghas often plays this tune in a lament-strathspey-reel set with "Niel Gow's Lament for the Death of his Second Wife" and "Captain MacDiarmid," most notably as his winning set in the Blairgowrie competition in 1969, which he won out of a field of 30 other competitors.— Ed.]

Daldowny's

Reel on A

Setting by Aonghas Grant

From the Uilleam Ross *Collection*, 1883. I think I play this one several different ways. Ross himself was a great one for changing tunes, even changing names. He was the second or third personal piper to Queen Victoria. He made pipes as well—I actually have a practice chanter made by him—it's the goose hanging now on the wall.

The Red Haired Girl of Tulloch

Strathspey on B

(♩ = 66)

Setting by Aonghas Grant

*1 - Bowing Performed:

*2

*3 - Transition to
"My Gentle Milkmaid"

My Gentle Milkmaid

Reel / Port-a-beul on B

(♩ = 96)

Setting by Aonghas Grant

Alastair Hardie and Aonghas at Stirling University, ca July 1985
[Photo by Della Matheson, from the archives of Janet Rae]

The Ale is Dear

Pipe Reel on B   (𝅗𝅥 = 100)

3rd & 4th Parts by Aonghas Grant
Setting by Aonghas Grant

This is an old reel. A setting was first written out from my playing by Renwick MacArthur. Renwick is a good friend who came to Stirling Summer School from the start. He wrote down a lot of tunes the way I played them. Renwick also plays pipes and double bass and has published a book of his own tunes, called *The Annan Collection*.

Aonghas working on a violin in his workshop at home in Lochyside

250 to Vigo

Reel on B

(♩ = 66)

By Angus R. Grant

Vigo [pron. "veego"] is a town in the north of Spain and 250 is a type of motorcycle. Angus Rory lived in Spain for a while, and he once got a ride to Vigo on a 250. This is a very popular tune now. [*Angus R. Grant is Aonghas' son, well-known as a remarkable fiddle player, a first-rate composer, and front man in the band Shooglenifty, which tours worldwide. The above tune was recorded on Shooglenifty's first CD,* Venus in Tweeds, *and it is played at a "half-reel" tempo.*–Ed.]

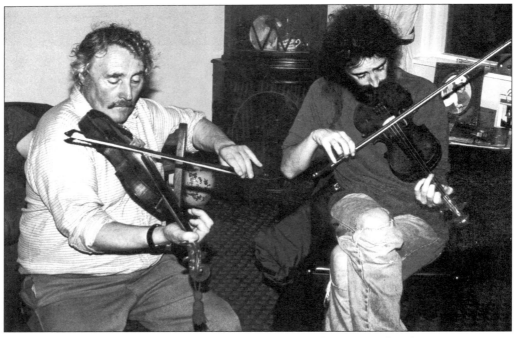

Aonghas Grant and Angus R. Grant jamming at home in Lochyside, 1999

Angus Grant, Rannachan, Lochailort

Strathspey on C

By Bert Murray (1913–2003)

From Bert Murray, the Auld Fiddler: "To wish the left handed fiddler Angus Grant every success. I hope the above tune will give you pleasure and mak' the rafters dirl."

I was at my brother's wedding, it was 1957, he married a lassie from Dyce. The band at the wedding—I bought them a round of drinks and said I was sorry I didn't have my fiddle with me. I didn't know anybody up there, I told them I was a fiddler myself, and he said, "Oh, have you heard of Bert Murray, he's a great friend of mine." I said I'd heard of him, I'd love to meet him. He said, "What are you doing tomorrow? Bert is staying in Aberdeen, I'll pick you up and take you to meet him." So that's how I met Bert the first time. He'd done this tune a day or two before, and he had no name on it, he gave it to me as a present. It was the only copy he had. I hardly met him again for years. About 40 years later I met up with him in California. He says to me, "Do ye still have this tune?" I said, "Aye, I'll make a copy." So he put it into *The Nineties Collection*. Rannachan is the estate I was working on when I met him.

A Mhaighdeannan a' Choire Dhuibh

"The Maids of the Black Corrie"

Strathspey / Port-a-beul on C

(♩ = 69)

Setting by Aonghas Grant

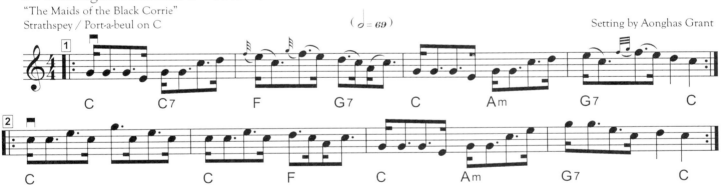

An old Gaelic port-a-beul. There are lots of black corries all over the place. A corrie is a hollow that's been gouged out by the glacier. It's not a glen; it's similar to a glen except that the top end is bowl-shaped. It's open at one end but closed at the other. If you go up the road here you'll see the corrie between Ben Nevis and Cairndearg. It's open at the bottom and steep at the top. There's coire dubh, coire buidhe—the yellow corrie, coire gorm—the blue corrie, coire glais—the gray corrie. And coire mòr, coire beag.

[This tune is very similar to The Marquis of Huntly's Highland Fling, often played as a strathspey in D, with the parts reversed.–Ed.]

Glengarry's Dirk
Strathspey on C   (♩ = 66)   Setting by Aonghas Grant

Loch Garryside
Reel on C   (♩ = 96)   By Archie Grant (ca. 1875–1948)
                                         Setting by Aonghas Grant

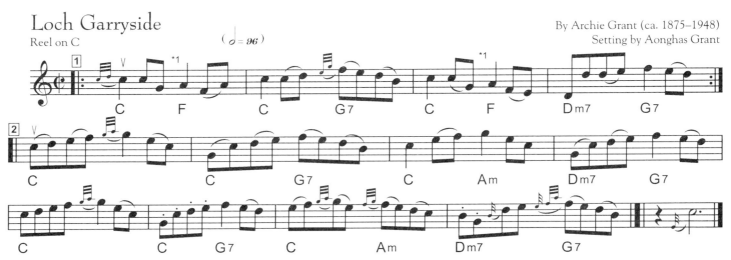

This tune was composed in 1908 or 1909. My uncle Archie was a fine piper and fiddler. Glengarry is the area where my father's family lived. It's just a bit north of here, and goes towards the west from the Great Glen. The loch is all different now, as it's been dammed up.

Archie Grant at the house at Glendoe, ca. 1935, with young Aonghas, Aonghas' younger brother Hamish, and Aonghas' mother Mary Grant

North of the Grampians

Strathspey on C

By Capt. Simon Fraser (1773–1852)

Setting by Aonghas Grant

*1 - Bowing Performed:

tip

*2 - Bowing Performed:

tip   long bows

*3 - Bowing Performed:

frog

The Haggis

Reel on C

By Capt. Simon Fraser (1773–1852)

Setting by Aonghas Grant

[This is a common Strathspey & Reel set in Scotland; Aonghas often plays these two tunes together, preceded by the slow air "Mrs Hamilton of Pencaitland" (see page 13), and won the Northern Counties Fiddle Championship in Inverness with this set in the 1970s.–Ed.]

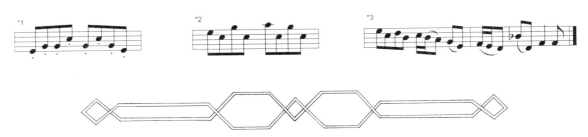

Clach na Cùdain

"Stone of the Tubs" ❖ The Key Stone of Inverness
Strathspey on D

Setting by Aonghas Grant

Clach na Cùdain is the key stone of Inverness. It is also known as the Stone of the Tubs, where the women rested their washing baskets after rinsing in the River Ness. There are different ways of playing this tune. You can add a lot of triplets. You hear a lot of dance bands playing triplets, particularly in the "Laird of Drumblair," which is one of Skinner's more popular strathspeys. It has a lot of triplets—you should never really play triplets for dancing, because it's confusing for dancers.

John MacDonald's Reel

By James A. Center (1879–1919)
Reel on D

Setting by Aonghas Grant

This is a popular tune with both pipers and fiddlers, and a favourite of Donald Riddell.

Cameron's Got his Wife Again

Strathspey on D

(♩ = 72)

Setting by Aonghas Grant

"Cameron's Got his Wife Again" is a very old tune; in Skye it is known as "Briogais Fhada Maighstir Ord," or "Long Trousers for Mr. Ord." Either way, it's a comical title.

The Red Burn

Reel on D

(♩ = 100)

By Aonghas Grant
Setting by Aonghas Grant

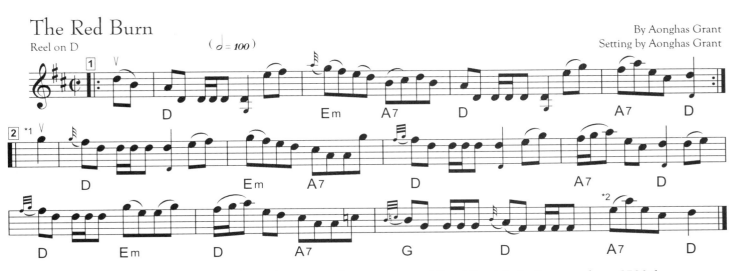

The Red Burn is the very steep burn that comes down in the middle of Ben Nevis. It starts about 2700 feet up in the rocks, and within yards it becomes a flowing torrent, there are waterfalls all the way down and in the wintertime it becomes an absolute flood. Nobody knows where it's coming from, it disappears into the rocks. It drops down into the River Nevis running through red granite, hence the Red Burn.

A Ben Nevis burn (stream)

Moch sa Mhadainn
"Early One Morning"
Strathspey on D

[This is very similar to a strathspey in Book 3 of Lowe's Collection called "Lord Eglintoune's Auld Man." It was published by Joseph Lowe in 1844.–Ed.]

Big Donald MacDonald
Strathspey / Port-a-beul on D & A   (♩ = 72)   Setting by Aonghas Grant

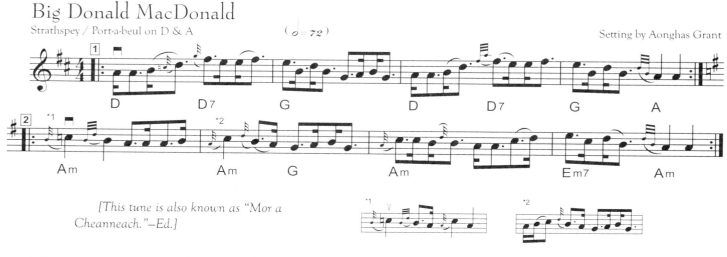

[This tune is also known as "Mor a Cheanneach."–Ed.]

Tha Bean Agam, tha Taigh Agam
"I have a Wife, I have a House"
Strathspey / Port-a-beul on D   (♩ = 69)   Setting by Aonghas Grant

This is a traditional strathspey, a port-a-beul, with Gaelic words. *[Aonghas plays another version of this tune on A. See page 68.–Ed.]*

Drochaid na Sìthiche

"The Fairy Bridge"
Reel on D

$(\textgreek{o} = 116)$

By Archie Grant (ca. 1875–1948)
Setting by Aonghas Grant

The Fairy Bridge is up Glenmoriston. It's collapsed now. This is the story my uncle told me: a long time ago there was a big storm, the river was in spate, there were no bridges, they couldn't get across for days. One of the Grants was walking up the glen, and he heard a wee voice in Gaelic saying, "Help me! Help me!" He looked and there was a wee fairy man trapped by his coattails under a tree that had come down. So he lifted the tree and the fairy said, in true fairy fashion, "I'll grant you one wish since you got the tree off me." He looked around, he looked at the river and said, "The river is fast, we can't get across it for days til it goes down—we need a bridge." The fairy man said, "You'll have a bridge in the morning." He went back and told people what the fairy told him, that there'd be a bridge in the morning. People came out, and they could see where there had been a bit of a waterfall at one time, now there was suddenly a big hole through the rocks, and all the water was coming out through the hole, and they could walk across this natural bridge. That's why they called it the Fairy's Bridge. The way my uncle told it, the tune describes the water coming through in jets, spouting through the hole. There may be no truth to the story at all, but apparently the bridge was there a long time. *[This was recorded on the LP* Highland Fiddle *as "Seann Drochaid," or "The Old Bridge."–Ed.]*

*1 - this is how Aonghas plays the 1st part of the second time through the tune on *Highland Fiddle*:

*2

*3

*4 - last two bars when ending

This is the first fiddle I ever started on. I got it from my uncle and I still have it nearly 60 years later. He was also left-handed. I have played that fiddle in the Assembly Rooms in Edinburgh, Inver-Lochy Castle, Airthrey Castle, and in Ireland. It's an old Scottish fiddle all battered up. It's been through the wars. It's got quite a nice back. I think at one time it had a label, 1836 or something like that.

Stirling Castle

Strathspey on D

By Prof. Charles Bannatyne (19th cent.)
Setting by Aonghas Grant

The Blairgowrie cups, 1969 & 1970

"Captain MacDiarmid" is the reel I played the first year at the Blairgowrie Festival. You played three contrasting tunes for the cup. Tom Anderson came down to judge and he put in the cup. There were 31 fiddlers—with the draw I was the 31st, the last one to play. I went across the street to a pub and had a big session with Hamish Henderson and the boys. About half past two this wee lassie came in and said, "Is Aonghas Grant in here—we're down to the second-last fiddler." So I told the boys "I'll be back—look after my drink." Tom Anderson was at the judging table, with Morag MacLeod assisting. Of course with so many fiddlers there was quite a lot of dross. Anderson said, "What are you going to play!?" I told him, "Niel Gow's Lament for his Second Wife," "J.F. MacKenzie of Garrynahine" and "Captain MacDiarmid." "How do you spell MacDiarmid!?" After I played I was getting ready to go back to the pub, and Morag MacLeod said in Gaelic, "You'd better stay." She knew I'd won it. In the announcement, Anderson said, "I've heard good fiddling, bad fiddling and indifferent fiddling! And the best fiddling I heard all day was the man who played with the corrie fist." He said he could hear the chanter sounding through the fiddle.

This was 1969. The next year Anderson judged it again and I won it again. Obviously he kept me in mind, as he phoned me up later, said "I'm thinking of starting up a fiddle school at Stirling and I want you to come down and teach." I said I'd never taught anyone in my life except my son. "That doesn't matter a dash. We'll have Shetland style, Northeast style, and the Highland style." If I hadn't gone down that day to Blairgowrie for the competition and played this tune, I probably would never have met up with Anderson, would have never been to Stirling and never started teaching.

Captain MacDiarmid

Aberarder Rant ❖ The Farmer's Daughter
Reel on D & B (from 1982 transcription) (♩ = *100*)
Setting by Aonghas Grant

Captain MacDiarmid

Reel on D & B (♩ = *112*)
Setting by Aonghas Grant

Captain MacDiarmid

Reel on D & B (from 2007 transcription) (♩ = *108*)
Setting by Aonghas Grant

[Here are three slightly different transcriptions of "Captain MacDiarmid." –Ed.]

85

Bear Creek Reel

Reel on D

(♩ = *100 – 132*)

By Aonghas Grant
Setting by Aonghas Grant

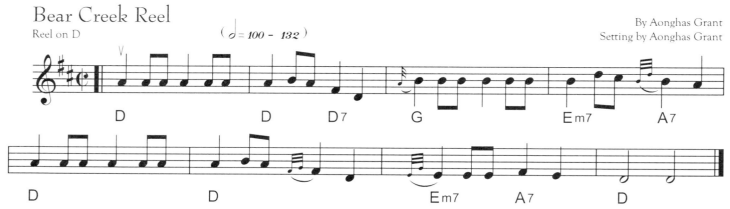

A very good tune for beginners. I call it the "Bear Creek Reel" because it's more American sounding. *[After playing it several times through at a walking tempo, Aonghas will typically pick up the speed, and add shuffle-bowing and drone strings to make it sound Appalachian.–Ed.]*

Roll Her on the Hill

Reel on D

(♩ = *96*)

Setting by Aonghas Grant

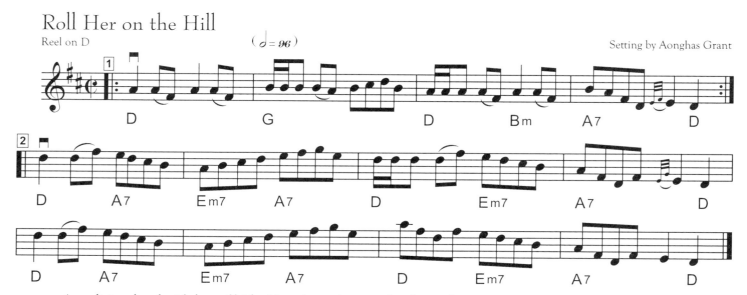

A traditional reel with lots of birls. It's quite a nice tune for the students.

Rachel Rae

Reel on D

(♩ = *96*)

By John Lowe (b. ca. 1765)
Setting by Aonghas Grant

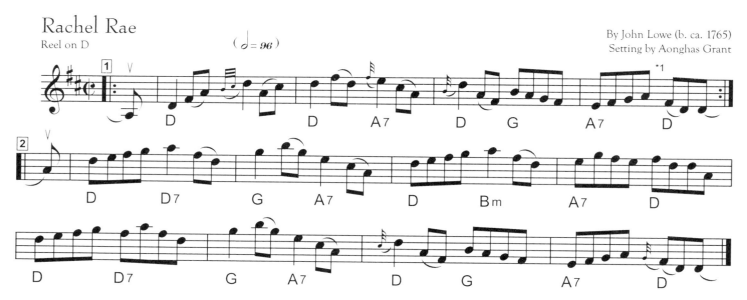

The double notes (2 eighths or quavers) are bowed together; the rest of the notes are "bowed out" (separate bows).

Belladrum House

Strathspey on D

(𝅗𝅥 = 69)

Setting by Aonghas Grant

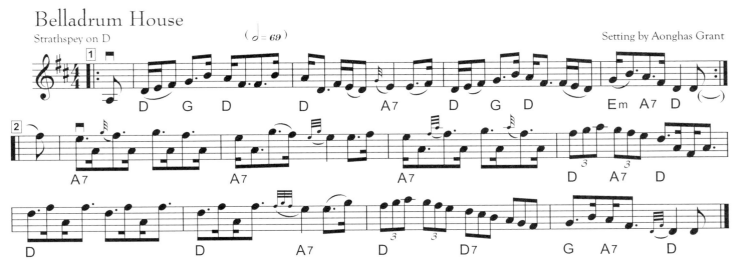

Belladrum House was near Beauly, in Lord Lovat's country. It no longer exists as it burnt down many years ago.

Greystone Park

Strathspey on D

By James Macintosh (1846–1937)

The Sound of Sleat

Reel on D

(𝅗𝅥 = 100)

By Donald MacKinnon (20th cent.)
Setting by Aonghas Grant

A pipe reel. The Sound of Sleat is the sound off the southern coast of Skye. "Sleat" is pronounced "slate." The Gaelic College, Sabhal Mòr Ostaig, is there. In a group of fiddlers, some might play the tune on the back strings—an octave lower.

*1 - bowing for beginning
of 2nd time through tune

*2

Moy's Reel

Reel on Eb

By Aonghas Grant
Setting by Aonghas Grant

For my wife, who has had nearly 45 years of having 3 fiddlers plus a piper in the family, as well as pupils trotting in most nights. They must be good players, as so far Moy has not left home. I don't often play in E-flat but I thought I'd make a special effort for my darling wife.

[The key of E-flat is indeed rare, as is Moira Grant, and we are very grateful to her for her Highland hospitality, generosity and perennial good cheer.—Ed.]

Moira and Aonghas with their granddaughter Eva, Lochyside, ca. June 2003

Mrs Charles Stewart of Pettyvaich's Reel

Reel on F

By William Marshall (1748-1833)

Rosemary's Reel

Reel on F

By Aonghas Grant
Setting by Aonghas Grant

To Rosemary Stewart, a Pupil and Friend. July 1984.

The Culachy Reel

Reel on F

By Aonghas Grant
Setting by Aonghas Grant

I spent a happy youth on the Culachy Estate as a hill shepherd among the deer and sheepdogs, with rifle and gun. What more could a young man ask for? Learned a lot about deer from John MacDonald.

Inchmagranachan
Strathspey on G

By James Macintosh (1846-1937)

Inchmagranachan is a place up by Dunkeld. Rosemary Stewart—of "Rosemary's Reel"—her people come from around there. Her father John was in a department at the University. They used to go caravan camping in the hills of Inchmagranachan. "Raineach" is the Gaelic word for bracken, so it could mean something like "Bracken Point."

Loch Ordie
Reel on G

By James Macintosh (1846-1937)
Setting by Aonghas Grant

"Inchmagranachan" and "Loch Ordie" are published in James Macintosh's rare 1930 collection.

Kincaldrum's
Reel on G

Setting by Aonghas Grant

90

The Laird o' MacIntosh
Strathspey on G
$(\text{♩} = 66)$

Setting by Aonghas Grant

From the Gow Collection. [This was published in the Athole Collection in 1884 as "Miss Douglas."–Ed.]

Perrie Werrie
Reel on G

Setting by Aonghas Grant

Perrie Werrie is a Scots expression for a child's spinning top, usually started with a whip.

Barbara Vander Muelin

Strathspey on G

By Aonghas Grant

Kees's Reel

Reel on G

By Aonghas Grant
Setting by Aonghas Grant

Barbara Vander Muelin is a good friend of mine, as is her husband Kees. Kees (pron. "case") is from Holland and came to the first Summer School at Stirling and to many others. We have been friends for over 20 years. They have a house in Lochaline and stay during the summers, and also for Christmas and New Year. Sadly, Kees passed away in 2006. He was probably the only Dutchman who could bow and play a strathspey.

Aonghas Grant, Stirling, ca. July 1985 [Photo: Kees Vander Muelin]

Miss Allison-Grace Taylor's Wedding

Strathspey on G

By Aonghas Grant

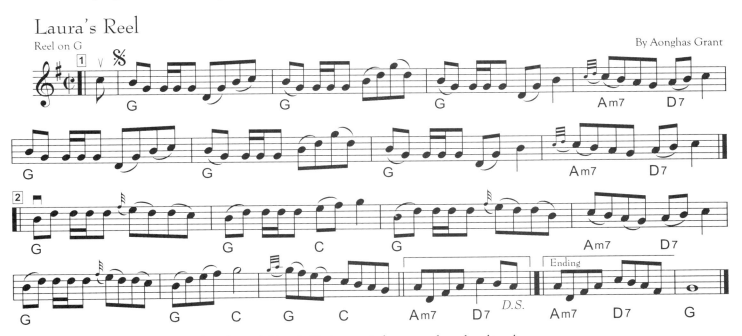

With every good wish for Allison-Grace on her wedding day, 10th September 1988. Allison-Grace is the daughter of friends Jessie & Joe Taylor; Joe Taylor is President of the famous Kingussie Shinty Club. The wedding was held in the Duke of Gordon Hotel, Kingussie; as this is the heart of the Strathspey District, the only suitable tune had to be a strathspey. The tune was originally transcribed by George Smith, the accordion player, while we were riding together in the car up to the wedding.

Laura's Reel

Reel on G

By Aonghas Grant

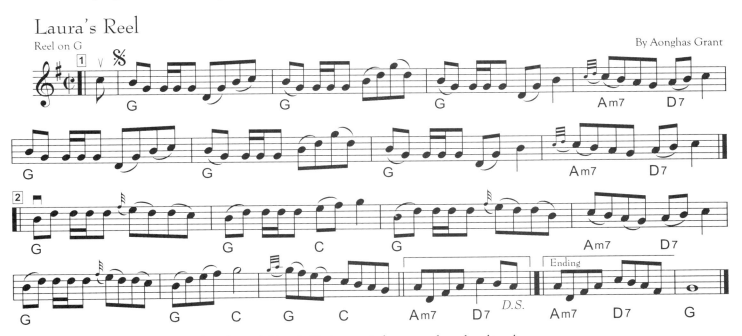

For Laura Young, a pupil and good friend. She's married now and a schoolteacher.

Aonghas with two young fiddle students, 2002, Lochyside

93

Munlochy Bridge
Strathspey on G   (♩ = 66)

Setting by Aonghas Grant

A pipe strathspey. Munlochy is in the Black Isle near Inverness. The Black Isle is a peninsula, with the sea on both sides, and the snow rarely lies there, hence the name. It is a fertile farming district.

Ruidhleadh mo Nighean Donn
"Reel of the Brown Haired Maid"
Pipe Reel / Port-a-beul on G   (♩ = 88)

Attr. D.A. Campbell (active 1894)
Setting by Aonghas Grant

"Ca' the Ewes" is the pipers' name for this tune. They usually play a 6-part setting.

Jigs

Rory MacLeod
Pipe Jig on A

By P/M Donald MacLeod (1917–1982)
Setting by Aonghas Grant

(♩. = 120)

Some people think jigs are not too important. Alex Grant, the great fiddle maker and leader of the Highland Strathspey & Reel Society, wasn't too keen on jigs. I think jigs are great fun. When you start off you play a lot of jigs, they're fun and easy to play, and you don't worry about making a mistake because you can play them like a slow air. It really gets the fiddle going. We used to play a lot of jigs for lancers and quadrilles. Now you don't see as much of that except among the Highland natives. There used to be about six sets—you stopped between each set, you give a chord, then you give another chord—it was very genteel, and you started off again. The great thing was to get turning so fast you could get the girl's feet clean off the deck. It was quite good fun. We used to play a tremendous mix of tunes, not specifically Highland tunes, but all sorts of tunes—Irish jigs, Tenpenny Bit, The Auld Gray Cat, The Drunken Parson, Sir Roger de Coverly.

Cailleach an Dùdain
"The Old Wife of the Mill Dust"
Jig on A

(♩. = 116)

Setting by Aonghas Grant

An old pipe jig. This was also a dance in its own right. I don't think anyone still knows how to dance it.

The Fraser's Jig
Jig on D

(♩. = 108)

Setting by Aonghas Grant

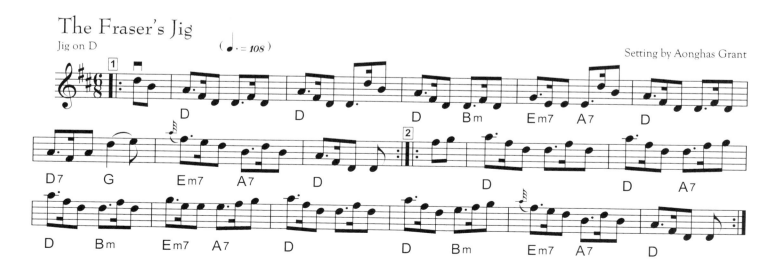

Cabar Fèidh

"The Deer's Antlers"
Pipe Jig on A

(♩. = 160)

Setting by Aonghas Grant

A herd of stags in the wintertime, Loch Arkaigside, 2007

Mèirleach Lochabair

"The Thief of Lochaber"
Jig on D

(♪. = 124)

Parts 3 & 4 by P/M Donald MacLeod (1917–1982)

Setting by Aonghas Grant

This was originally just a two-part tune and the great piper Donald MacLeod added the third and fourth parts to it. The Thief of Lochaber wasn't your commoner garden thief, this was one of the great cattle thieves that probably went on one of the big cattle raids down south. This was quite a recognized way of life in the Highlands. The young men would go down south to Stirling and Crieff and, in the dark nights without the moon, they'd steal the cattle and swiftly take them up north, and into the glens for the summer, and quite cheekily go back in the fall of the year to the markets in Crieff and Falkirk, and sell them back to probably the same farmers they'd stolen them from. Rob Roy MacGregor did a lot of that they reckon, and there also was a protection racket. The drovers would go down armed to the teeth with the famous Doune pistols, and the Highlanders would charge them a fee through their part of the country to save themselves from attack.

Aonghas sometimes
reverses the bowing
on the repeat of a part.

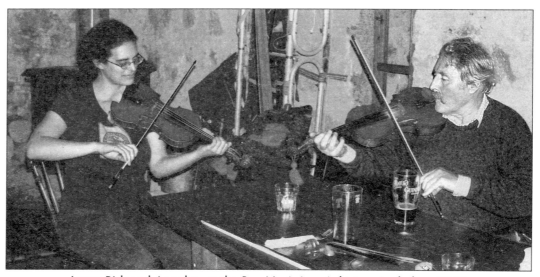

Laura Risk and Aonghas at the Ben Nevis Inn, Achintee, Lochaber, 2005

98

Over the Border

Jig on D

By Sue Jones
Setting by Aonghas Grant

Seconds—Over the Border

By Catriona Thompson

By kind permission of my friend Sue Jones, who lives in Chester, England, and has been a stalwart at Stirling University Summer School. This is quite a different style of jig, being English.

The Maids of Edrachaolis

Jig on A

(♩. = 108)

Setting by Aonghas Grant

A pipe jig from the far north-west. *[This tune bears some similarity to the 6/8 pipe march "Cock o' the North."—Ed.]*

The Black Haired Girl of Knockie

Jig on A

(♩. = 124)

Setting by Aonghas Grant

*1—The birls in the 1st, 3rd and 5th bars of the 2nd part are played just like birls in reels; here the 2 sixteenths and eighth figure (2 semiquavers and quaver) takes the place of 3 eighths (quavers).

*2

A pipe jig from the Uilliam Ross *Collection*, 1869. Knockie is an estate in Stratherrick. It was owned at one time (1700s into 1830s) by Capt. Simon Fraser, who called his music collection by that name. Fraser by some bad deals lost the estate and latterly lived in Rose Street, Inverness, and died in rather poor circumstances. At one time he had been a wealthy landowner. His natural son Angus Fraser collected some of his father's manuscripts which were lost for a long time, and found only in recent times. They were published for the first time, in 1996.

Hector's Jig

Pipe Jig on A

(♩. = 124)

By Hector MacFadyen (20th cent.)
Setting by Aonghas Grant

This tune is from John MacFadyen's collection, and Hector is his brother. The MacFadyens are one of the great piping families of Scotland.

An Cruinnèachadh Iomlan Lùthmhor

"The General Gathering"
Jig on D

(♩. = 108)

Setting by Aonghas Grant

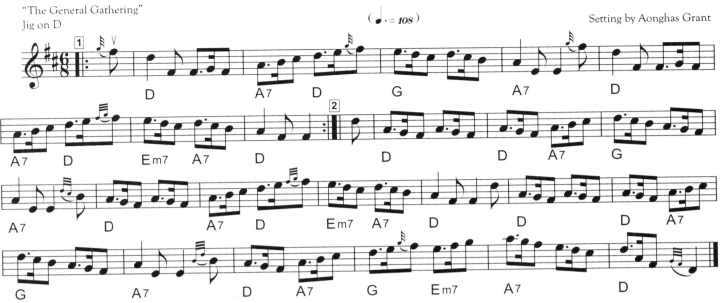

The "General Gathering" was the raising of the Standard at Glenfinnan, August 19, 1745.

Glenfinnan Monument, Lochaber

Morgan Rattler's Jig

Jig on D

(♩. = 104)

Setting by Aonghas Grant

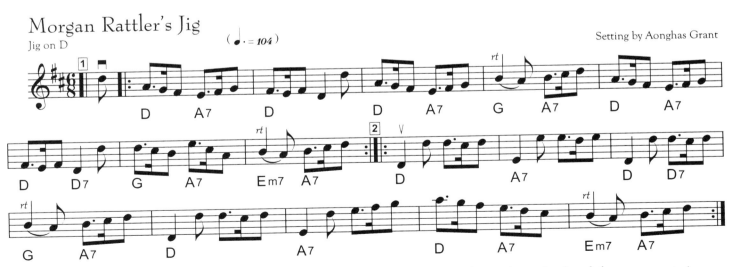

A traditional jig, found in Gow and other collections. It has more parts but we've only played these two parts in the Highlands.

Dì-moladh an Uisge-bheatha

"In Dispraise of Whisky"
9/8 Jig on G

(♩. = 112)

Attr. John Murdo MacRae (d. 1775)
Setting by Aonghas Grant

G   G7   C   G   Em   D7   G   G7   C   Am   D7   G

G   C   G   C   G   D7   G   C   C   G   D7

G   Em   D7   G   G7   C   G   G7   C   Am   D7   G

Iain Murchadh MacRath (John Murdo MacRae) was the factor for Lord Seaforth up in Kintail and also was a famous bard. He was at a wedding in Kintail in the 1760s and got very drunk. Some days later he met the local preacher who rebuked him for being drunk and not a good example to the young men of the Glen. Iain said he would compose a song running down drink. It was obviously done with tongue in cheek because it turned out to be a jig. Most of the words are lost now but the few I've heard from some of the old-timers, it was a tremendous song—he was running down whisky in one sense and it was getting praised up in the other. "Whisky was such an evil thing it would make you dance like the lambs in Spring and things like this," and "Whisky how can you make me dance with the young maidens as if I were a young man."

A few years later most of his friends were going away to the Carolinas, and though he was a fairly wealthy guy, being Factor to Lord Seaforth, he decided to go with them. He got to the sailing boat in Kyle, and while they were waiting for the tide to turn, he invited the Captain to have a meal with him. Smoked salmon, wine, all that—the Captain was amazed, and said, "Do you always eat like this at home?" He replied, "Fairly often." "I advise you to stay where you are then!" After he got to the Carolinas, he composed a few songs, then the American War of Independence started. All the Scots were told to line up and sign an oath of loyalty to the King, German Geordie. They weren't allowed to leave, and the Highlanders were all forced against their will to don the Red Coat and fight. He was killed in one of the first battles. The Scots must have been in a terrible bind, because they had signed an oath, and in those days your oath was your bond, you wouldn't go against it, even though it meant you'd put on the Red Coat and fight with the English against the American rebels.

*1

Ciamar is urra' sinn Fuireach on Dram

"How can we abstain from whisky" ❖ The Legacy
9/8 Jig on G

(♩. = 104)

Attr. John Murdo MacRae (d. 1775)
Setting by Aonghas Grant

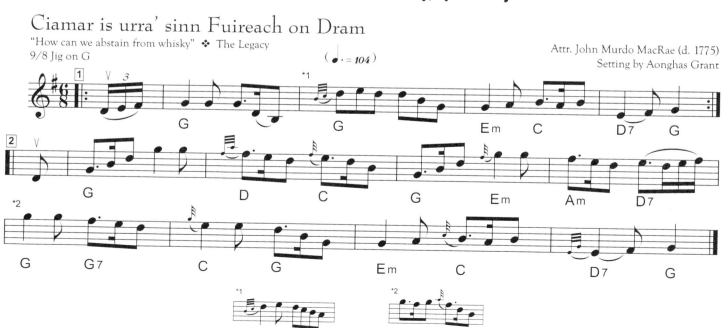

G   Em   C   D7   G

G   D   C   G   Em   Am   D7

G   G7   C   G   Em   C   D7   G

*1   *2

102

Ho rò mo Bhobag an Dram

"The Favorite Dram"
9/8 Jig on G

Attr. Alasdair MacDonald of Moidart (ca. 1695 – ca. 1770)
Setting by Aonghas Grant

A traditional jig, collected by Capt. Simon Fraser. This is also a well-known Gaelic song. One of the best versions is sung by the well-known singer / piper Ruairidh Peter Campbell, from Barra.

The Coffee Break Jig

Jig on G

By Aonghas Grant
Setting by Aonghas Grant

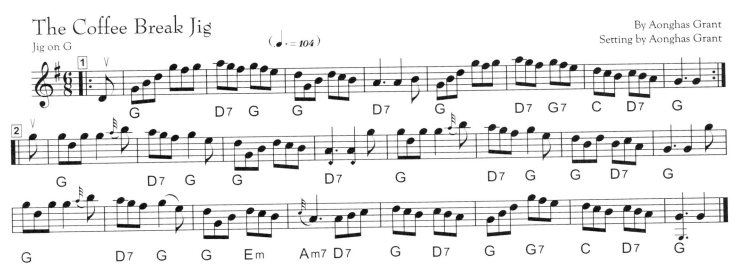

Stirling University, Easter 1985. The story goes—at Stirling they used to have this powdered coffee, and a boiler thing for hot water. They used the cheapest of cheap coffee there, it was absolute rubbish. The only way we could drink it was to put a wee shot of whisky in it. We used to keep a half bottle or two of whisky in the piano, because we never used the piano. One afternoon Robert Innes, the Director, appeared with a woman, apparently a famous pianist, who said she'd like to join us for a tune. We all thought about the two half-bottles of whisky in the top of this upright piano. Two or three of the boys in the class rushed up to offer to shift the piano over, and while they were shifting the piano they managed to slip the bottles out. That was a good thing—the bottles would have jammed up the piano.

Jock's Fiddle

Jig on G

By Aonghas Grant
Setting by Aonghas Grant

(♩. = 108)

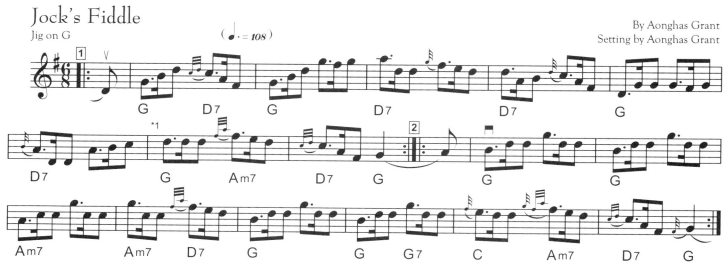

Jock Kirkpatrick was a great friend of mine—we had long days in the hills together. He was a sheep manager across the river from ourselves. He'd lost an eye in his young days and even with his one eye he was a great sheep man and a great rifle shot and gun shot. He used to go on a motorbike and played the fiddle at dances. Sometimes we'd go down to a sheep sale in Inverness and I used to come back with him on the motorbike. He had the disconcerting habit of speaking to you and turning all the way round to see you with the only eye. He was a great character, so I composed a jig for him, on his fiddle. This was composed when I got Jock's fiddle from his widow a number of years ago.

*1

Aonghas on his motorbike, ca. 1962

This was the last motorcycle I had—I paid £70 for it. They're a collector's item now, worth at least £2000. Moira had a go-round on it when we were courting. As she rounded the corner she nearly ran into her father with his sheepdogs.

Hornpipes

The World's End Hornpipe
Hornpipe on D

By Sue Jones

The World's End is a pub down in Chester, England.

Sue Jones, Stirling, ca. 1983

The Marquis of Lorne Hornpipe

Hornpipe on G   (♩ = 76)   Setting by Aonghas Grant

The Mariner's

Hornpipe on D   (♩ = 72)   By Aonghas Grant
Setting by Aonghas Grant

This is one I made called the Mariner—the seaman. There's a friend of mine from boyhood named Hugh Dempster. He was in the Merchant Navy for a long long time, and they called him the Mariner. I composed this one for him.

Aonghas and John Campbell on the ferry Outward Bound,
Boston Harbor, August 2003

106

The Westcoaster

Hornpipe on G

By Aonghas Grant
Setting by Aonghas Grant

There's absolutely no tradition of hornpipe playing in the Highlands at all. There's not one single hornpipe. So this is the original, first one. It's dedicated to the West Highland Fiddle Class at Stirling University. It was originally transcribed by Rosemary Stewart. Hornpipes are very, very nice tunes to play because most of them are uncomplicated, although they can be fancy, like the "Beeswing" and "Newcastle."

"This is more a west coast of the mind, rather than any particular place."—Moira Grant

[Watercolor "The Day Before Tomorrow" by Moira Grant, 2002]

This page has been
intentionally left blank.

Related Collections

Bremner, Robert. 1751-1761. *A Collection of Scots Reels or Country Dances With a Bass for the Violoncello or Harpsichord.* London: Robert Bremner, 96 pp.

Bryan, Valerie. 1996. *Ceòl nam Feis.* Portree: Fèisean nan Gàidheal, 103 pp.

Bryan, Valerie. 2000. *Ceòl nam Feis 2.* Portree: Fèisean nan Gàidheal, 115 pp.

Dunlay, Kate and David Greenberg. 1996. *Traditional Celtic Violin Music of Cape Breton.* Toronto: DunGreen Music, 158 pp.

Fraser, Capt. Simon, ed. 1816. *The Airs and Melodies Peculiar to the Highlands of Scotland and the Isles.* (Also known as *The Knockie Collection.*) Edinburgh: Printed and sold for the editor, 113 pp.

Glen, John. 1891. *The Glen Collection of Scottish Dance Music.* Edinburgh: Glen, 48 pp.

Glen, John. 1895. *The Glen Collection of Scottish Dance Music, Book II.* Edinburgh: Glen, 50 pp.

Gow, Nathaniel, ed. 1819. *The Beauties of Niel Gow, being a Selection of the most Favorite Tunes from his First, Second, and Third Collections of Strathspeys, Reels, and Jigs, Chiefly Comprising the Compositions of Niel Gow and Sons.* Parts 1-3. Edinburgh: Gow and Galbraith, 38 pp. each part.

Gow, Niel. 1784-1822. *A Collection of Strathspey Reels, etc...* 6 vols. Edinburgh: Niel Gow and Sons, 36 pp each vol.

Hardie, Alastair J. 1992. *The Caledonian Companion.* 3rd edition. Edinburgh: Hardie Press, 144 pp.

The Inverness collection of Highland pibrochs, laments, quicksteps and marches, carefully & effectively arranged for the pianoforte, and containing some of the most popular and favorite airs of the Highlands of Scotland. c1900. Inverness: Logan & Co., 62 pp.

MacDonald, Keith Norman. 1887. *The Skye Collection of the Best Reels and Strathspeys Extant, Embracing over four hundred tunes collected from all the best sources, compiled and arranged for Violin and Piano.* 3rd edition, 1980. Sydney, Nova Scotia: Cranford Publications, 195 pp.

MacDonald, Keith Norman. 1895. *The Gesto Collection of Highland Music.* Leipzig, 187 pp.

McDonald, Patrick. 1784. *A collection of Highland vocal airs, never hitherto published. To which are added a few of the most lively country dances or reels of the North Highlands & Western Isles: and some specimens of bagpipe music.* Reprint edition, 2000. Isle of Skye: Taigh na Teud Music Publishers, 76 pp.

Neil, J. Murray. 2005. *The Scots Fiddle: Tunes, Tales and Traditions of the Western Highlands, Hebrides, Orkney and Shetland.* Glasgow: Neil Wilson Publishing, 242 pp.

Ross, Uilleam. 1885. *Ross's Collection of Pipe Music.* Edinburgh: Wood & Co., 254 pp.

Robertson, James Stewart. 1884. *The Athole Collection of the Dance Music of Scotland.* Edinburgh: JS Robertson. Reprint edition, 1961. Edinburgh: Oliver & Boyd, 318 pp.

Discography

Grant, Aonghas. 2008. *The Hills of Glengarry.* Shoogle Records 07006.

Various artists. 2001. *From Sea to Sea: Music and Memory along the Caledonian Canal.* The Highland Council.

Grant, Angus, Angus Ruairidh Grant and Farquhar MacRae. 1980. *Port an Dubh Ghleannach–Traditional Highland Fiddle Music.* The Ardkinglas Trust AAT1.

Anderson, Tom, Aly Bain, Angus Grant, Alastair Hardie, Bill Hardie, Hector MacAndrew and Donald Stewart. 1980. *The Fiddler's Companion.* Legacy Recording 03CD.

Grant, Angus. 1977. *Highland Fiddle.* Topic 12TS347.

Website

Aonghas Grant - www.scottishfiddle.org/angusgrant

Further Reading & Listening

Alburger, Mary Anne. 1996. *Scottish Fiddlers and their Music.* 2nd edition. Edinburgh: Hardie Press, 256 pp.

Bruford, Alan and Ailie Munro. 1973. *The Fiddle in the Highlands.* Glasgow: An Comunn Gaidhealach, 12 pp.

Cannon, Roderick D. 1988. *The Highland Bagpipe and its Music.* Edinburgh: John Donald, 203 pp.

Collinson, Francis. 1966. *The Traditional and National Music of Scotland.* London: Routledge and Kegan Paul, 294 pp.

Collinson, Francis and Peggy Duesenberry. 2001. "Scotland §II: Traditional music." In *The New Grove Dictionary of Music and Musicians,* 2nd edition, ed. Stanley Sadie. Vol. 22, pp. 908-922. London: Macmillan.

Cooke, Peter, ed. 1989. *The Fiddler and his Art.* Scottish Tradition Series, no. 9 [LP]. Tangent Records, for the School of Scottish Studies, University of Edinburgh. CD Reissue: Greentrax CDTRAX9009

Cowie, Moyra. 1999. *The Life and Times of William Marshall, Composer of Scottish Traditional Music & Clock Maker and Butler to the 4th Duke of Gordon.* Elgin: Almac Printed Ltd., 115 pp.

Dickson, Joshua. 2006. *When Piping Was Strong: Tradition, Change, and the Bagpipe Tradition in South Uist.* Edinburgh: John Donald, 256 pp.

Eydmann, Stuart. 2006. "Unravelling the Birl: Using Computer Technology to Understand Traditional Fiddle Decorations." In *Play It Like It Is: Fiddle and Dance Studies from around the North Atlantic,* ed. Ian Russell and Mary Anne Alburger, pp. 33-41. Aberdeen: Elphinstone Institute.

Gore, Charles, ed. 1994. *The Scottish Fiddle Music Index.* Musselburgh, Scotland: The Amaising Publishing House Ltd., c500 pp.

Grainger, Percy. 1908. "Collecting with the Phonograph." *Journal of the Folk Song Society* 12, pp. 147-242.

Lockhart, G. Wallace. 1998. *Fiddles and Folk: A Celebration of the Re-emergence of Scotland's Musical Heritage.* Edinburgh: Luath Press Ltd., 139 pp.

MacDonald, Fergie, with Allan Henderson. 2003. *Fergie: Memoirs of a Musical Legend.* Edinburgh: Birlinn, 175 pp.

MacLean, Calum I. 1990. *The Highlands.* Edinburgh: Mainstream Publishing, 224 pp.

MacLeod, Bobby. 1984. *Pas-de-Bas: A Pot-Pourri of Facts, Thoughts and Opinions about Dancing and Music in Scotland.* Kilmacolm, Renfrewshire: John Littlejohn Publications, 51 pp.

McMillan, Shona. 2008. "A Highland Gentleman: The Roshven Fiddler Farquhar MacRae." *Fiddler Magazine* 15(1), pp. 12-17.

Munro, Ailie. 1996. *The Democratic Muse: Folk Music Revival in Scotland.* Rev. ed. Aberdeen: Scottish Cultural Press, 248 pp.

Purser, John. 1992. *Scotland's Music: A History of the Traditional and Classical Music of Scotland from Earliest Times to the Present Day.* Edinburgh: Mainstream Publishing in conjunction with BBC Scotland, 311 pp.

Shepherd, Robbie. 1992. *Let's Have a Ceilidh: The Essential Guide to Scottish Dancing.* Edinburgh: Canongate Press, 101 pp.

Smout, T.C. 1986. *A Century of the Scottish People, 1830 - 1950.* London: Fontana Press, 318 pp.

Text Index

Tune Index

Tune Index (cont.)

Barbara McOwen, Laura Risk and Peggy Duesenberry, Stirling, 2005

Barbara McOwen was encouraged by Scottish country dancers in the San Francisco area in 1971 to play for dancing. She drew on her dancing and music experience, her library of books and recordings, her A.B. in Music from the University of California at Berkeley, and the growing local folk music community, and formed a band, The Berkeley Scottish Players, which exposed a number of dancers and musicians to the Scottish repertoire. The band recorded three landmark LPs during the 1970s. After moving to Boston in 1979, Barbara established the dance band *Tullochgorum* and co-founded several community Scottish music ensembles and the Boston Harbor Scottish Fiddle School.

Peggy Duesenberry is a fiddler and ethnomusicologist, with a PhD in Music from the University of California, Berkeley. Her main research area is Scottish fiddle music, and she was awarded a Fulbright Scholarship for her doctoral research on broadcasting and Scottish fiddle tunes. In 1997, she began teaching at the Royal Scottish Academy of Music and Drama in Glasgow, first as Course Leader for the BA (Scottish Music) and now as Lecturer in Ethnomusicology. Peggy has designed and taught courses in fieldwork, transcription and analysis, and both historical and contemporary studies in Scottish music, and she supervises PhD students.

Laura Risk grew up in the thriving San Francisco Scottish fiddle scene of the 1980s and 90s, learning her craft from fiddler Alasdair Fraser. Now living in Montreal, Laura tours internationally as a soloist and with her band Triptych. She has over ten albums to her credit, including her latest release *2000 Miles*, which offers a distinctly Québécois take on classic Scottish fiddle tunes. Laura is also active as a record producer and she recently completed a five-year tenure as an Instructor of Fiddling at Wellesley College. Laura is currently a graduate student in Musicology at McGill University.

The Glengarry Collection Vol. 1

The Highland Fiddle Music of Aonghas Grant

Performed by Aonghas Grant, Fiddle

DVD Volume 1 • NTSC • Standard View 4:3 • Zones 1-8
Mel Bay Publications Inc. •• www.melbay.com

TUNES

Cut out and fold for DVD insert

118